William Jewett Tucker

The Making and the Unmaking of the Preacher

Lectures on the Lyman Beecher Foundation, Yale University, 1898

William Jewett Tucker

The Making and the Unmaking of the Preacher
Lectures on the Lyman Beecher Foundation, Yale University, 1898

ISBN/EAN: 9783337144340

Printed in Europe, USA, Canada, Australia, Japan

Cover: Foto ©Lupo / pixelio.de

More available books at **www.hansebooks.com**

THE MAKING AND THE UNMAKING OF THE PREACHER

Lectures

ON THE LYMAN BEECHER FOUNDATION

YALE UNIVERSITY, 1898

BY

WILLIAM JEWETT TUCKER

PRESIDENT OF DARTMOUTH COLLEGE

BOSTON AND NEW YORK
HOUGHTON, MIFFLIN AND COMPANY
The Riverside Press, Cambridge
1898

TO

THE YOUNG MEN

WHO HEARD THESE LECTURES

CONTENTS

LECTURE	PAGE
I. Preaching, under Modern Conditions	1
II. The Making of the Preacher by Education	31
III. The Unmaking Process	61
IV. The Preacher and his Art	90
V. What the Preacher owes to the Truth	116
VI. What the Preacher owes to Men	145
VII. The Pulpit and the Church	169
VIII. The Optimism of Christianity	198

THE
MAKING AND THE UNMAKING OF THE PREACHER

I

PREACHING, UNDER MODERN CONDITIONS

EACH new incumbent of this Lectureship can but feel the increasing stringency of the situation. Twenty-five courses of Lectures on Preaching have now been delivered on the Lyman Beecher foundation. Doubtless one who ventures upon another course may count upon the good will of his predecessors, but he quickly learns that they have done nothing to lighten his task, but rather everything in their power to make it difficult. The one source of inspiration and courage to each Lecturer, in his turn, is the presence and coöperation of men, who, in their turn, have come to feel, in the separateness of their own first experiences, something of the responsibility and joy of preaching. I thank you, therefore, for your assuring welcome.

Allow me an opening word in regard to the significance of a subject in such a course of lectures as that now before us. A subject, to borrow the homely analogy of our Lord, seems to me to be like " the leaven which a woman took and cast into three measures of meal till the whole was leavened." It is the idea, the personal idea, which one casts into the common stock of opinions and experiences and beliefs, and it is to be measured altogether by its quickening and pervasive force. It is not good as a subject beyond its power to leaven.

I am proposing to speak to you about The Making and the Unmaking of the Preacher. That is my subject. Outside its reach I have nothing to say about preaching. My subject places us in the discussion, as you see, under the limitations of the personality of the preacher. We are also to remember that it gives us the freedom of his personality.

How shall we really put ourselves within so great a matter as that of preaching? Where is the point of reality? I know of no place where one may so certainly expect to find it as in the consciousness of the preacher. Around him and above him stretch the vast ranges of truth. They all contribute something to his message. Before him is the common humanity. Nothing which belongs to that can be alien to him. But neither truth nor man has anything to do with preaching until each has found the rightful place in the consciousness of the preacher.

Here, then, you have the method as well as the reason of my subject. I am intent upon finding out and taking the measure of those forces which are steadily at work toward the making or the unmaking of the preacher, because they are actually determining at any given time the value of preaching. Some men are preaching better at forty or at sixty than when they began; others are not preaching as well. The unmaking process is going on side by side with the making process. Some of the forces which are acting in either direction are altogether personal; others are too general to be of much account. We say that there are preaching ages, ages which furnish at once the message and the listening ear. We say that there are ages which are lacking in stimulus and in response. I think that we make far too much of these contrasts. I believe that it is one part of our business to reduce these variations to a minimum. If there is anything which should move on from generation to generation in the consistency of power, though it should be as flexible and elastic as the spirit of man, it is the Christian pulpit.

I do not propose to enter into any definitions of preaching. These have their legitimate place in the class room. But having chosen a subject which lays the stress so largely upon personality, I cannot afford to pass by the question — Who, under present conditions, is the Preacher? I address myself to the answer of this question in the opening lecture.

There are a great many ways in which we can discriminate the preacher from other men of like general aims or methods. We can say that he is like this man in the use of method, though unlike him at every other point; or that he is like that man in the object which he seeks to accomplish, though unlike him in other respects. Let us make no account of these likenesses or contrasts, but rather try to find what is necessary to enable one to meet the present conditions of preaching. Whether the preacher has much or little in common with men of like callings is for our purpose a matter of indifference. How shall we name the preacher of to-day by his actual work?

It may not be saying the greatest thing, but it is saying something very much to the purpose, as I conceive, when I insist that the preacher of to-day is the man who is able to enlist other men in his work of persuasion. He is the man, that is, who is able to make his audience preach with him and for him. Jesus alone with the woman at Jacob's well was the preacher. Paul and Silas were preachers in the jail at Philippi. But they were not preaching under modern conditions. An essential, one is tempted to say, a supreme condition of modern preaching, is an audience. Modern preaching is so far conditioned upon an audience that the argument for the pulpit above the press, as an agent for the effective communication of truth, rests very largely upon this condition as a premise. Why should a man go to church when he can stay at home and read a sermon? Put aside the necessity for worship, and what answer can you make? It is hardly safe to risk the argument upon the assumed advantage of the spoken above the written word. That advantage depends upon the effect of the spoken word, not simply upon one's self as an individual, but also upon the whole body of which he is a part. It is indeed quite conceivable that the spoken word may find a lodgment in the heart of one hearer, when all others are untouched. The written word usually has a better fortune. But the highest efficiency of the spoken word may be far above that of the written word. The power of preaching, I insist, that which is natural and legitimate to it, is the power to reach the one through the many. It is the power to bring the consenting reason and the awakened conscience and the kindled emotion of the whole to bear upon every part. You can easily test this principle. You find yourself in an inattentive congregation, or, if it is formally attentive, unawakened and unkindled. The state of that congregation is a hindrance to your reception of the truth. You expend a good part of your power of reception in resistance to the general indifference. You find yourself in another congregation. The mood is eager and expectant. The congregation knows the preacher and is ready for him. Before he has uttered a word you are in a measure committed to him through those who have learned to feel his power.

Every person who attends church may be made to answer a twofold purpose. To the degree to which he is receptive he thereby becomes influential. He is a communicating force. In fact he may actually communicate more good than he receives. I doubt not that in every congregation there are those whose chief virtue lies in the fact that through their quick sensibilities they are distributing agents of the truth.

It is this possibility of using men as his allies in the interest of righteousness which constitutes one of the chief attractions of the pulpit to men of what is known as popular power. There is a true philosophy in the vulgar, commercial test of a preacher, — "Can he draw?" Drawing men means that the preacher is utilizing them. They may not be conscious of it. Some of them, if they knew it, might deny the fact. Still the fact remains. It is the reason for their presence.

If you ask me in what this power of the preacher to utilize an audience consists, or why it is that one man can make an audience preach with him more than another, I do not intend to be beguiled into any detailed answer. The personal gift which is usually offered in explanation of personal power is always insufficient and often misleading. But I will give one answer, without prejudice to what I may wish to say hereafter, which seems to me to be most inclusive. The power of a preacher to reach the individual through the audience is usually in proportion to the depth and breadth of his humanity.

The great preachers have various personal characteristics. Some have humor, and therefore pathos, and others have neither. Some are men of presence, others are not. Some speak, others read. Some are thinkers, others speak to the limit of the last thought. But, without an exception, all within my knowledge who stand the test of compelling others to join with them in their work of persuasion are men of tremendous humanity.

What do we mean by humanity when we apply it as a quality to the individual? Certainly it is something very different, as a qualifying term, from the adjectives which come out of the same root. To say that a man is human is to suggest some weakness or fault, on which we look with leniency, if not with tenderness. We like to draw our great men a little nearer to us on the common ground of shortcomings and imperfections. It was not on the whole an unpleasant discovery when the American people found out that Washington had a vigorous vocabulary. And when we go a step further and say that a man is humane, we simply apply to him a term of advanced civilization. We mean that he has the great qualities of justice, tolerance, and charity. But when we speak of the humanity of an individual, we refer, I think, to the amount of human nature which is to be found in him. It is a word of amplitude, a term of inclusiveness, standing over against everything which is narrow or hard or thin, as well as against mere artificiality and conventionalism. We naturally turn for our chief example to that great impersonality, Shakespeare, who, however elusive he may have been in himself, held in his imagination every type of human nature, and whose creations are therefore as secure in the life of the world as are the men of its own history. Or we turn to our own Lincoln, whose personality when measured at this point seemed almost as great as that of the nation. I doubt if the national conscience ever carried a heavier burden of justice than that which weighted his soul. Recall Emerson's word about him, spoken at Concord on the day of his burial, — " He *is* the true history of the American people in his time. Step by step he walked before them, slow with their slowness, quickening his march by theirs, the true representative of this continent, an entirely public man, father of his country, the pulse of twenty millions throbbing in his heart, the thought of their minds articulate in his tongue."

Humanity then, according to our understanding of it, is something quite beyond any of the terms which are identified with it. It is in every way to the advantage of the pulpit that ministers are now understood to be human. When it was accepted as a qualification for the ministry that one was not a man of like passions with others, or when the ministry itself was considered as offering special exemptions from temptation, it must have been a terrible ordeal to preach. I cannot conceive how a man could stand in the presence of his fellow men and speak right out the words which should fall into the midst of temptation and struggle, and at the same time feel that his words might stir the question in any man's heart,—what do you know about it all? where are your temptations? Let us be thankful for the recognition of the human in the profession of the ministry. And of course it goes without saying that ministers are supposed to be a humane class, notwithstanding the occasional bloodthirstiness of the pulpit in times of national excitement.

But the humanity of the pulpit, its power to cover in thought and feeling the life before it, to stand for the common nature, to be so far able to represent men that it can turn them to its own uses, that is something which waits full recognition, because it is something which needs to become more evidently the fact. I was careful to say when I began to speak about this matter, that the ability of the preacher to make other men help him, to make his audience preach for him, might not be the greatest condition of modern preaching which one has to satisfy; but the more we dwell upon what this ability implies, the more we shall be disposed, I think, to advance the claim. Nothing can be more fundamental to the preacher than his humanity. There lies the priestly quality of his life. And just as the wants and desires and aspirations of men go sweeping through his humanity when he intercedes for them with God, so through that same channel God's message returns to them. Preaching at its best is prayer turned round. " Now then we are ambassadors for Christ, as though God did beseech you by us: we pray you in Christ's stead, be ye reconciled to God."

It may seem to you, however, that I put myself on clearer and firmer ground, when I say that if one is to satisfy the conditions of modern preaching he must be able to show that he has a sufficiency of truth in actual command. Of course this means the authority of the pulpit. I desire to say with the greatest possible emphasis that modern preaching waits the word of authority. There is a good deal of preaching which is not modern, which uses the authoritative language and tone. On occasions, as it passes into controversy, it deals in anathemas. But these are manifestly futile. An assertion of authority which wakens the protest of the devout reason or reverent scholarship of an age fails, because it lacks one of the chief elements of authority. Authority cannot rest upon the impossible or the unreasonable, or upon what may be to most minds the merely external. When, therefore, men of recognized spiritual power choose to plant themselves upon the literalism of Scripture, they are accepted by the majority of their hearers for what they are in themselves, not for what they say. Their life may preach to all, and it may be a glorious message; but the interpretations, the criticisms, and the arguments in which they trust for conviction, meet none of the conditions of authority.

But because a good deal of the authority which the pulpit assumes is misplaced, it by no means follows that we have enough of it. On the contrary, I reaffirm the statement that the mind of the age is ready and anxious to come under the authority of truth. What proportion of men do you think wish to reason God out of existence or out of his world? How many are longing to disbelieve in immortality? How many of those even who break the commandments wish to abolish them? How many would prefer to have Christianity proven a myth rather than an historic fact? Let us not wrong the temper of our age, however much we may share in its mental perplexities. I am confident that nothing would receive so true a welcome from the mind of this age as some great vindication of religious faith — the equivalent in our time of Butler's Analogy, or of Edwards on the Will. It is no disproof of this opinion to say that we stumble over the creeds and confessions. We forget that the ages which produced these symbols had the advantage of us in that these symbols were their own productions. The age which produces the next great confession will take delight in it, and repeat it in sincerity, it may be in triumph.

Meanwhile, however, we must remind ourselves, in justice to the fact, that faith has not been left amongst us without its witnesses. If pressed too hard, our age may reply to any age of the creed, " Show me thy faith without thy works, and I will show thee my faith by my works." The same faith which wrote the confessions is busy on mission fields, in hospitals, and in schools. It is no more to the discredit of faith to be obliged to confess that it is now more practical than intellectual, than it is to the discredit of genius to be obliged to confess that it has gone over so largely into invention, and become the slave of utility. And yet, I think that I cannot be mistaken when I note the growing desire and disposition of men to come again under the sway of great intellectual beliefs, to come again under authority. This is no retrograde movement. It is not a call to rest. It is rather, as I interpret it, the appeal of the intellect to be allowed to go out once more into the affirmative, and to take the open field in behalf of spiritual truth. We have given over a long generation to criticism, to discussion, and to readjustment in the region of theological beliefs. Darwin published the "Origin of Species" in 1859; Jowett, the "Essays and Reviews" in 1860; and Colenso, his views on "The Pentateuch" in 1862. From that time on English-speaking Christendom has been engaged in investigation or controversy. There has been no waste of time. There is no reason now for impatience. Neither truth nor righteousness is ever in haste. As Charles Sumner used to say, "Nothing is settled till it is settled right." But as the power of the pulpit depends upon the sufficiency as well as upon the certainty of truth, there is coming to be a popular demand for an increase in the volume of acknowledged truth. Measured by the formalities of the creeds, there has been a large shrinkage. Has there been in reality a shrinkage? Has there not been an extension of natural and revealed truth — if in using these terms we keep to the old distinctions — in all directions? Is not the thought of God larger, closer, more pervasive than ever before? Does not Jesus Christ hold a more fundamental and central position than he held at the time when Christianity began to be reëxamined? Is the Bible less true in its new freedom than when it was in bondage to inerrancy and infallibility? Are the problems of human destiny less serious or awful because studied in the terms of a larger Christianity. Surely if we are straitened, it is not in the truth, it is in ourselves.

I do not underestimate the work of a generation just emerging from a period of criticism and controversy. We must be patient. No progress is made by running in advance of facts. But there comes a time, we are always to remember, when the pulpit anticipates the schools. Great truths announce their presence before they are formulated. They are tried, proven, experienced, before they are ready for the confessions. The proclamation of the incoming truth always precedes by necessity and therefore by right the formulation of it. This has been the history of the great doctrines. The deity of our Lord, and in due time his humanity, justification by faith, the sovereignty of God, the universality of the atonement, were all apprehended and declared by the clearer and braver souls before they became the doctrines of the church. It is at the dawn, before a truth has faded into the light of common day, that the preacher has the rare, inspiring authoritative opportunity. Let no man be deceived by the shallow dictum, — the true is not new, the new is not true. Truth is always coming into the world under conditions which make it for the first time clear and imperative. Then it is as new as if it had not always existed. It was justification by faith on the background of penance, indulgences, and superstition, which gave us the Reformation. It was the sovereignty of God over against spiritual tyranny in high places which gave us Puritanism. It was a universal atonement made necessary by the unanswerable appeal of an opening world which gave us modern missions. It is no less evidently true that the immanence of God could not have come into the real apprehension of the world until modern science had prepared the way for it; nor that the conception of the Kingdom of God on earth could have really become a hope and an expectation until men had begun to see, as in our time, the capacity of human society, and had begun to feel, as we are feeling, those strange and well-nigh universal yearnings for the brotherhood of man. The process is always going on. It is the divine method to bring out truths, to force them to the front, to make them new. Blessed are the ages in which the work is most evident. Blessed are the men who at such a time have vision.

> "Then felt I like some watcher of the skies
> When a new planet swims into his ken:
> Or like stout Cortez when with eagle eyes

> He stared at the Pacific — and all his men
> Looked at each other with a wild surmise —
> Silent, upon a peak in Darien."

But you may say to me, every preacher, as he begins his work, has something more than the uncertainties of his time to contend with. He has the uncertainties of his own mind. How then can he have authority? Dr. Dale quotes the saying of a young friend, " A minister, when he is just beginning to preach, must sometimes write a sermon to clear his own mind on a subject." To which he adds the shrewd remark, " A sermon which is written to clear the mind of the preacher will be very likely to perplex and confuse the minds of the hearers." " It would strike you as very odd," he goes on to say, " if a politician told you that he had made a speech in Congress in order to clear his own mind on the true economical doctrine about money." No, that particular exhibit would not strike us as very odd, but, barring the illustration, we will take the principle.

I may be pardoned if I refer to an experience of this sort in my own early ministry. I had prepared a sermon which had been, I doubt not, profitable to me, but which was so utterly ineffective as a sermon that I took the liberty of asking a very discerning friend what was the difficulty with it. His reply was the best criticism I ever received. "You seemed to me," he said, "to be more concerned about the truth than about men." Yes, that was the difficulty. I saw it in a moment. I had no right as a preacher to be concerned about the truth. I should have had the truth in command, so that I could have given my whole concern to men. As it was, the sermon lacked authority.

It is not so practical a question as we may at first suppose — how far can the preacher be a searcher after truth and yet be the preacher. A searcher after truth he must be to be the preacher. The preacher ought to have the two qualities of freshness and fullness. I have recently listened to a course of lectures from one of the really great teachers of our time, a man characterized by both these qualities. He told, I think, the secret of his power, when he chanced to say in conversation,

"Every day's lecture should stand for what a man might say, as well as for what he does say." It is the unsaid word, if we know it is there, it is the sense of power in reserve after one has done his best, it is the absolute certainty of mental and spiritual growth, which give a people confidence and grateful delight in a preacher.

But a preacher must learn to guard the processes of his mind so that he can think not only forward but backward: backward, that is, toward what is most fundamental and even elementary in truth; for it is there that he makes sure and deep contact with the mind of his audience. "What is eloquence," Vinet asks, "but the power of the commonplace? It is making the primitive chords vibrate." Great fundamental truths have this power: unquestioned and unquestionable truths, that go from heart to heart, never denied access or hospitality, and never enfeebled by use. The more of these truths the preacher has in command, the more he will be able to realize what I spoke of at the beginning, the preaching power of an audience. A truth of this sort when once it is in full play between the preacher and audience, how good it is to be either preacher or hearer! Hearing is then the answering voice. Preaching and hearing — it is "deep calling unto deep."

Grant that the preacher of to-day has humanity and authority, that he has the power to compel men to help him in his work of persuasion, and that he has a sufficiency of truth in command, what does he lack, if he lack at all, in meeting the conditions of modern preaching? Is there any other quality, which is a peculiar necessity of our age, and which, because of this necessity, the age has the right to demand of the pulpit? I answer unhesitatingly, yes: the preacher of to-day must have faith. He must be able, that is, to give men elevation and outlook.

One cannot fail to see when looking at our time from a spiritual point of view, that it is not only self-absorbed, but self-centred and self-sufficient. We have broken the connection with other times. We are living in the isolation of our knowledge, as others may have lived in the isolation of their ignorance. We are so much to ourselves that we have rejected the companionship of the past, and are not anxious or even curious about the future. Of course, this is a kind of provincialism; just as the resident of a great city is apt to be bounded by it to the degree by which he is enlarged by it. The average Londoner or Parisian or New Yorker lives more in his city than in his country. He is not so sensitive to the national spirit as his neighbor is who is less overpowered by his immediate surroundings.

It is not to be wondered at that the average mind which is in and of this age is bounded by it. Not only is there more of the world than at any previous time, but most of the things in the world are worth more. One cannot calculate by just how much the valuation of the world is increased. This is not necessary. The moral effect of this increase lies in the appeal which the world of to-day makes to sense rather than to faith. In spite of the great contrasts in material condition, no one can mistake the satisfaction which men take in the material world, as they know it, as they possess it. With some it is a purely sordid gratification, the mere sensual enjoyment of prosperity. With others it is the satisfaction which comes from the opportunity of search and struggle, the hot competition of the business world. With others still it is the joy of investigation and physical research, the pursuit of knowledge for the sake of knowledge. We cannot overestimate the fact that the world, this physical world, means more to us than it ever meant to living men. Never before did men possess so many lands or subdue so many seas. Never before did men know so well the secret of wealth. And never before have there been opened to them so many provinces in the invisible realms of matter.

Now it is not difficult to see that soon or late there will be a spiritual reaction from this intense satisfaction in what we call the world. I do not mean simply a reaction from low and sordid worldliness, but from all which the material world has to offer. The soul of man cannot live upon the income of material wealth. The soul of man cannot live upon the discoveries of science.

Extend the world as you will, there is no lasting satisfaction in it for the human soul. And when the time of spiritual dissatisfaction comes, — no one knows how near it is, — then we have this alternative, either the return to some kind of other worldliness, or the advance into some more spiritual conception of the world itself. I cannot believe in modern mediævalism. I must believe in such a spiritual interpretation of this world, and in such a spiritual use of its forces as will satisfy the souls of men.

But, meanwhile, the problem of the preacher is how to lift men above their time for spiritual uses, how to give them elevation and outlook. You may be surprised when I say that one of the greatest incentives to faith in such a time as this is the historic spirit. Here lies the interpretative power of faith. Balaam was right when he said of Israel, " Israel has no need of diviner or soothsayer: it is enough to say in Israel, what hath God wrought." The men of our time must be made to see and to know their place in the long plan of God. We need to go back far enough to get the grade on which the world has been moving, to feel the ascent in the providence of God. The increasing argument for faith lies in history. It is the great argument against narrowness, against complacency, against low outlooks. It lifts the spiritual horizon.

When we think of the peculiar office of faith we naturally turn toward the unseen. One of our first questions is about immortality. Can the preacher make that real to men to-day? Yes, but not in the same way as at some other times. This world is not the same as when the contrast was first made between it and heaven. The outlook into the future from Rome under Nero was very different from the present outlook from England and America. Persecution offers no spur to hope. The Christian centuries have made this world more desirable. We can hardly sing, except under some spiritual exaltation, the hymns of mediæval saints as they turned their hearts heavenward. It is not possible therefore that immortality can make its appeal in precisely the same way to us as to them. It is no longer the appeal of one world against another. What is the present significance of immortality? It is the appeal to the soul of man in behalf of its rights both here and hereafter. Immortality means more and more the spiritual, not only that which outlives time, but that which cannot be satisfied with the things of time. The faith of the preacher shows itself therefore in the clearness, in the urgency, and in the expectation with which he addresses himself to the spiritual man. If he does not himself see the things of the spirit here and now, and believe in them, he has scant vision for such an age as ours. If he does see these things, if men as they come and go before him are more to him in their souls than in their outward estate, whatever it may be, they too may have power to look at the greater and imperishable self, and come under the power of the vision now made their own.

But there is another way of elevation and uplift which is open to the preacher according to his faith. I believe that it is in some respects more possible to make Christ real to men than it is to make their own souls real to them. And if there has been any advantage from the distractions to the pulpit during these past years, it has been in the unanimity and urgency with which the pulpit has turned to the person of Christ. It is the wider and more familiar knowledge of Christ, which, more than all else, has held our age to faith. Men could not utterly disbelieve in his presence, they could not deny the Kingdom of God which he set up on the earth, they could not despair of themselves, when they saw the possibilities of their own nature revealed in him. There are altogether insufficient ways of preaching Christ, but I doubt not that even through these many have been led to touch the hem of his garment and have been made whole. It is given to the individual soul to claim the right of its full salvation in Christ. That obtains at all times and in all places. It has been given to our age in a very real and very peculiar sense to be saved, as an age, by the presence of Christ. It is his presence which has made it possible for the spiritual to live in the midst of the tremendous materialism of the century.

I think that I have said enough in these opening words to show you my conception of the preacher as he undertakes his work under present conditions. Modern preaching puts the emphasis on the humanity of the preacher, on his authority, and on his faith. He must have power enough over men to make them help him; he must have some sufficient truth in absolute command, that is, he must be possessed by it; and he must have some vision of the spiritual, which, at the highest, as at its nearest, is the vision of Christ.

Do the conditions seem to you to be hard? They are none too hard for the greatness of the work, nor for the joy of its reward.

II

THE MAKING OF THE PREACHER BY EDUCATION

IN the opening lecture, after considering the motive and reason for our subject, we passed at once to the question, Who, under present conditions, is the Preacher? Modern preaching, as we saw, lays the emphasis upon the humanity of the preacher, upon his authority, and upon his faith. The questions which it is asking all the while, and with the greatest solicitude about every man in the pulpit, are these: Does he compel other men to help him in his work of persuasion: does he make his audience preach for him? Has he a sufficiency of truth in command: does his preaching rise to the stress of a gospel? Is he reaching the spiritual man who is in bondage to the material wealth of the age: is he able to give elevation and outlook to those about him?

These questions, as we judged, revealed the inexorable conditions of modern preaching,—hard conditions, we granted, were they not matched by the greatness of the preacher's task, and by the joy of accomplishing it.

There is another question which lies upon the threshold of our discussion. It is so much a part of our inquiry into the Making of the Preacher, that we cannot afford to pass it by. How far can we expect to educate the Preacher?

I address myself to-day to the answer to this question, premising that it is in no sense limited to the training in our seminaries.

We are met at the outset by the classification in some minds of the preacher with the poet and orator, as born, not made. Let us not altogether ignore this classification. The preacher may be the poet or the orator, according to his birthright. And to the extent to which he justifies either claim, it is to be admitted that there is a personal element which is a law unto itself. " Genius," John Foster says, "lights its own fires." The independence of genius is to be acknowledged. If any considerable part of those entering the ministry or any profession bore the unmistakable mark of genius, I confess that our systems of education would be strained to make room for them. Somebody has asked what chance Carlyle would have in a modern university. Tennyson refers with little satisfaction or gratitude to his student days at Cambridge. It is not enough to reply with the cheap sarcasm that it will be sufficient time to consider this matter when the number of Carlyles and Tennysons entering our universities is appreciable. We are not to trifle with the personal element in any man. It is as sacred to society as to the individual. I concede that it must be allowed the largest freedom which it can show a right to, and that it must be put under the full stimulus to which it is entitled. Education cannot be conditioned in mediocrity. It must have regard to the exceptional as well as to the average man. Indeed, there is an increasing reason, which I will adduce in a moment, why I think that in the training or recruiting for the ministry especial regard should be had for the exceptional man. We are beginning to recognize the fact that in the interest of the social economy, for the very necessities of society, we must draw upon the widest sources of intellectual supply, and open the way out toward all the unknown possibilities of genius. Let me quote the word of Professor Marshall in reference to the large duty of education at this point, assuming that what he says has its proportionate application to the use of opportunity and incentive toward the ministry:

"The laws which govern the birth of genius are inscrutable. It is probable that the percentage of the children of the working classes who are endowed with natural abilities of the highest order is not so great as that of the children of people who have attained or have inherited a higher position in society. But since the manual-labor classes are four or five times as numerous as all other classes put together, it is not unlikely that more than half of the best natural genius that is born in the country belongs to them; and of this a great part is fruitless for want of opportunity.

There is no extravagance more prejudicial to the growth of national wealth than that wasteful negligence which allows genius that happens to be born of lowly parentage to expend itself in lowly work. No change would conduce so much to a rapid increase of national wealth as an improvement in our schools, and especially those of the middle grades, combined with an extensive system of scholarships, which would enable the clever son of a working man to rise gradually from school to school till he had the best theoretical and practical education which the age can give."

Now the special reason for consideration in behalf of the ministry, of the unknown or exceptional man, lies in the change which has taken place in the outward incentives toward the ministry. Under the New England traditions the ministry was an aristocracy, and therefore had the social incentive at work for its supply. Family life was set toward it. It passed as a profession from father to son. Children were consecrated to that form of service, and not infrequently bore names to remind them of their high calling. Mr. Beecher used to say that "none of the boys in his father's family ever thought of trying to get away from the ministry, except one, and that he made no such success in his waywardness as to encourage the others to attempt to follow him." The ministry of that time was more than a profession, it was a class. Our non-conformist brethren from England who visit us think that traces of this distinction still remain.

And as the family life was set toward the ministry, so was the higher education. College after college arose, that "the light of learning should not go out, and that the study of God's word should not perish." If one wanted the best education, he must find it in the courses leading to the ministry. These were full and abundant. They had the acknowledged right of way. They moved on in easy confidence to the remotest bounds of theological learning. The contract with the first professor of languages in Dartmouth College ran as follows: " Mr. Smith agrees to settle as professor of English, Latin, Greek, Hebrew, Chaldee, Syriac, etc., in Dartmouth College, to teach which and as many of them and other such languages as he shall understand, as the trustees shall judge necessary and practicable for one man, and also to read lectures on them as often as the president and tutors, with himself, shall judge profitable to the seminary."

We may not say, perhaps, that the change in regard to these two early incentives to the ministry is equally great. The tendency of the family toward the ministry is probably still stronger than that of the school. But from both directions the change is very manifest. And the compensation for this change is in the fact that in place of these intermediate influences we have now the more direct appeal of the ministry to the individual man. More men are to-day, I believe, entering the ministry of their motion than at any previous time. I have in mind not a few candidates who are making their way into it out of hindering and diverting surroundings. I see those in our colleges who want to cross the lines of study that they may put themselves into connection with a theological training, indicating that the earlier direction was unadvised. I take account of those who are leaving other professions while it is yet early enough to study for the ministry. Nothing, I think, impressed me so much, when in the service of a theological seminary, as the number and the quality of men who had turned to the pulpit out of mature conviction, and under purely personal and independent incentives. I am convinced that the recruiting ground of the ministry must be more and more among undesignated, uninfluenced, unknown, and exceptional men. The ministry must find its recruits, like any calling, among those who are so minded; only that in this regard it has the mighty advantage, in the case at least of the exceptional man, that he is consciously and imperatively called of God.

As we pass then to the direct question, How far can we educate the preacher? we must keep in mind the fact that education no longer makes a favorite of him. The favorite now is the student of science. The larger increase of subject matter, the accepted method, and the enthusiasm from discovery and from application, are to his especial advantage. So it appears. But I am not sure that it is really any more to his advantage than it is to the advantage of the preacher. In any event what matters it whether we be favorites or not? Who wants more than his opportunity?

Education, meaning by it that organized system which is now open to every one, can do these three things to make ready the preacher:

First, it can do more than at any previous time to develop and furnish the man, provided he has insight and patience. The old education, which specialized from the beginning straight toward the ministry, produced some very clear and noble results, the like of which you may see to-day in the Romish priesthood. It was an education with clearly prescribed ends, which were reached by clearly prescribed methods. But something often seems to be lacking in the lives of those who came under that training, and sometimes the lack is pathetic. We are aware that the whole man is not always before us. Some part of the nature is untouched, or if touched undeveloped. Occasionally we get a hint of what the life might have been under a broader or freer training. Does any one suppose, after reading Jonathan Edwards' study of the spider, that it would have been a loss to theology if he had opened his mind wide to the study of nature? To the extent to which we allow ourselves to be less than we are capable of being, we make ourselves of less use to society. Society wants the full man, the live man, the sincere man. I do not refer to the after straightening which may come to every one. The first business of education is to make sure that the discovery of one's self is reasonably complete. And at this point modern education can serve the preacher better than the old, provided, I have said, he be patient. Impatience, haste, will neutralize the larger opportunity. It is the danger which confronts every one to-day in the process of education. The contention is now stoutly urged that the schools deliver too late into life, therefore the time of preparation must be abridged. I take issue, in behalf of the ministry, with the premise. As Mr. Greeley replied to the man who demanded a job of him on the ground that he must live, — "That remains to be proven."

Why should one take less time to enter upon those callings which are preceded by what is known as an education, than to enter upon those callings which are preceded by an apprenticeship? Mark Twain has stated the present business situation in an aphorism, — "No occupation without an apprenticeship; no pay to the apprentice." In what business may one expect to find himself thoroughly established, with influence or authority in the firm or corporation, with a generous income, and possessed of a home, while as yet he is within the twenties? Is it in banking, or in manufacturing, or in railroading, or in general trade? How much farther along is the man of business at thirty than the lawyer or doctor at that age, unless he has unlimited capital or is of exceptional capacity? The open fact is, that society is growing more complicated, its demands are more exacting, and consequently personal advancement is slower. As surely as the rate of interest is declining, so surely are we all coming under the law of diminishing returns; which means that for the same results we must do harder work or secure a better equipment, which in turn means that we must take a longer time in preparation. I see no reason, therefore, why a man who proposes to enter upon his life work by way of an education should complain of the time required to prepare for it, and especially in view of the fact that the working time of life has been greatly extended. If society calls a man later to his tasks, it allows him to remain longer at them. The age of retirement has been advanced. Whatever the young man in his impatience seems to be losing reappears in the unspent force of later years.

A second result to be expected from modern education — I cannot overestimate its value to the preacher — is that it can give him contact with the mind of his time. Without question the minds of men are finding their chief training to-day in the school of utility. When Thoreau graduated at Harvard — it was about sixty years ago — he made the statement in his graduating address "The world is more beautiful than useful." That is a statement which no one could dispute then or now. Every one's opinion must depend upon his point of view. But whatever may have been the proportion in Thoreau's time, it is now evident that where one sees real beauty in the world, ten see more clearly some kind of utility, and without doubt the proportion is increasing.

Here then is a vast amount of mind to be reached, some of it thoroughly trained. It does not follow that a preacher must therefore become a utilitarian in his thinking. It does not follow that he must use the motives which lie on the low plane of utility. It does follow that he has an immense advantage if he knows and understands through his own training the working of this kind of mind. For one thing, he will not offend and alienate it by inexact methods of thought. His statements will bear verification. His arguments will hold true to the laws of evidence. Having made contact with the mind thus trained, he will be able to move to his own ends. Imagination, sentiment, emotion, will not be wasted. Exact thinking is not opposed to high thinking, nor logic to feeling, nor carefulness of speech to the freedom of the imagination.

I have a practical suggestion to offer to our seminaries. I find that there is a considerable number of men who have been trained in the scientific or semi-scientific courses in our colleges, who wish as they near the close of their college course to study for the ministry. Usually they are men of assured strength. Their decision shows that they are of mature and independent mind. No motive could influence men in these conditions except the overruling desire to enter the ministry. What can be done for them? They will bring strength and consecration to the pulpit. They will be a special power in bringing the pulpit into contact with the type of mind which we have been considering. I do not hesitate to ask for a place for them in our seminaries, in our best seminaries, and that facilities be offered them for gaining the necessary technical knowledge, especially in Greek. Otherwise we shall lose, out of the trained ministry at least, more and more of the best mind which our colleges are producing.

The third result which education ought to be expected to give to the preacher is the clear and sure access to truth. Not possession of it in any large degree, that is the work of a lifetime, but access to it.

I desire, gentlemen, to enter my protest and warning in your presence against the assumption that truth in any form can be had for the asking, that it lies within easy reach of the mind. That is never the fact. Truth there may be within us or above us, written "on the black bosom of the night," for the guidance of our feet in plain paths; but that is not enough. The paths of men are no longer plain; they cross and recross in bewildering confusion; the world thickens; and he who makes too easy a thing of duty or of truth only adds in time one more bewildered or wayward soul to the care of the great shepherd and his church.

In spite of what we rightly call progress, in spite of the great and sure gains of knowledge, in spite even of revelation, nothing is more evident and more impressive than the remoteness of truth from each new age. What is it which calls out the finest energy of each new age except the search after truth? This is no pastime. It is the serious business of serious men, lovers of their kind as well as lovers of truth. Who are scholars, and what are they trying to do? Men who want to know the truth, the whole truth, and nothing but the truth, and who want to have their fellow-men know, as they know, that, as Descartes said, "they may walk surefootedly in this life."

It is well to remind ourselves of these motives and aims of all true scholars, and of the urgent necessities which rest upon them, in view of the still remaining attitude of a part of the church towards its most advanced scholarship. We cannot do too much to correct the mistake in many honest minds, that scholarship creates confusion, and introduces doubt where before there was faith. And to make this correction, we must show how simplicity of thought and life has given way to complexity, which means that much hard, brave, patient thinking must be done by somebody in every department of life before anybody can act. There never was a time when the motto of Governor Winthrop, of Massachusetts Bay, was more pertinent than now — "When you don't know what to do, don't go and do it."

In fact, it has now become evident that there are but two valid positions for the church to take, to fall back upon authority and go to Rome, or to encourage all clear, straight, honest, reverent search after the truth. The truth we want and need and must have for the ordering of faith and the conduct of life is not so accessible that we can dispense in the least degree with scholarship, unless we are prepared to accept authority. The most serious business therefore in the education for the ministry is to give to the men who are to assume its responsibilities access to the truth. If there is any distinction between an educated and an uneducated ministry, it is here: not simply that one man can use better English than another, or quote more authors, or answer men with quicker wit, but that the educated preacher can give light, restore confidence, guide more safely and farther, and if need be take command when there is a call for a spiritual leader.

You do not ask me how this access is to be gained. You are in the process.

I cannot forbear, however, a word as to the range of the work. The same kind of eager but patient thought is needed in every department of theological training. The Bible is no more inaccessible to us than to our predecessors, when measured by the separating effect of language; but it does offer a more arduous task to us, since we have undertaken to find its place in history, and more than that, to put ourselves within its great historic order and movement, and let it carry us along according to the providence of God.

It is no easier task when we turn to theology, when we consider either what the Bible has to say, or nature. Nature seemed to the theologian of the past generation simplicity itself. Our fathers preached Paley's Natural Theology as easily as they preached the Levitical law. They may not understand the embarrassment of those who must now take account of the theory of Evolution, but they have no right to say to us, after this long and pleasant experience in the use of "Paley," that the pulpit has no further use for what they called natural theology. There is no option about the use or disuse of truth.

And when we turn to our social problems, we find ourselves under no less a necessity for painstaking and thorough study. The difference between the old philanthropy and the new, or between the lower and the higher, has been well put in the statement, " The lower philanthropy tries to put right what social conditions have put wrong: the higher philanthropy tries to put right the social conditions themselves." The difference is immense. It is the difference between the charity which expresses itself altogether in relief and rescue and the charity which expresses itself in restraint and precaution, in the effort to rescue the rights of the individual, and in the greater effort to effect at some vital points the readjustment, if not the reconstruction, of society. If the good is the foe of the best, then it is true that there is a sense in which the old-time charity hurts the new. As Jacob Riis said a little time ago in a convention, in which the scripture "Charity covereth a multitude of sins" had been made to do its accustomed work, — " Brethren," speaking with his Danish idiom, "it was time to take that cover off."

Whichever way, then, we turn in our present work, we see that education puts the newer demands upon us, and offers us everywhere the new privileges. We get much in method: we get something in actual results: we get more in the sense of the strain and toil which truth demands, no, I will not say demands, but allows, of those who are to use it for the good of their kind. Is there not an unmistakable joy to-day in the companionship of scholars, an exultation in the atmosphere of scholarship?

These three things we ought to expect of education as an organized system, which takes a man up on his way to the ministry: it ought to develop him and furnish him as a man, not simply as a preacher; it ought to give him contact with the mind of his time; and it ought to give him access to the truth; not the means simply, but the strenuous spirit of search.

I would like to devote the remainder of this lecture to the somewhat informal consideration of certain influences, which, though not strictly and technically educational, are operative within the period of education.

Among these influences which I have in mind, I put first the influence of some one person, be he instructor or author, upon the mind and heart of a student. In the old version, there stood out in the margin of the book of Malachi a phrase which expresses by a happy turn what I want to say. The phrase has been incorporated into the new version, but in the change its power as a definition has been lost. God was threatening, as one of the penalties of disobedience, that He would cut off from Israel master and scholar. The margin said, "For master and scholar read, ' him that awaketh, and him that answereth.'" That is the influence I have in mind as I speak, the influence of "him that awaketh" upon "him that answereth." It is something beyond the constant impression which comes from good teaching. It is the spark, which at some fit moment is dropped into the nature, which is ready to be kindled.

As these lectures allow personal experience, I will recall an illustration from my own life. Near the close of my seminary course, when I was in no little doubt about the reality of what I had to preach, and was therefore hesitating between the law and the ministry, I chanced upon the " Life and Letters of Robertson." One letter which caught my attention contained a statement of his personal feeling toward Christ. I had never known till then that a man could feel in just that way about Christ. Here at last was reality. It gave me what I wanted. I began at once on my own account the study of the life of Christ. I began with the temptation, the point I judged of greatest reality to him. And from that time on I had no question about the ministry. Robertson, with his passionate loyalty to Christ, wakened the answering passion in my soul.

There are many ways in which this more personal influence may be expressed. One man is able to impart something of the quality of his own thought to the thinking of those who come under him. The virtue which goes out of him lies in a certain sentiment which spiritualizes his thought. This imparting of the quality or sentiment of one's mind may mean more in the way of personal influence than a founding of a school of disciples. The influence of Coleridge was, I judge, of this order. It held together many minds which differed widely in their theological positions. Another form of influence may be traced to those who deal in method or impression, to those who are distinctively preachers, whether they are thinkers or not. In times just gone by, we recall at once Mr. Beecher and Mr. Spurgeon. The influence of these men was profoundly spiritual and ethical, albeit it produced as a secondary result not a little imitation on the part of those who could not look below their methods into their spirit. But the chief influence which comes to us from helpful men is that which comes to us straight out of their personality. They may be thinkers; they may be distinctively preachers: we do not refer to them in either capacity: we call them by name. So we speak of Maurice, and Robertson, and Kingsley, and Bushnell, and Brooks. These, and the like, are men who touch us, and we are most sensitive to their touch in the days of our preparation for the ministry, especially if for any reason our thinking or our plans go wrong.

Next to the stimulus of the "master," whoever he may be, I put the contagion of the group,—the influence of the associated life of which one is a part during the process of education. Education in its earlier stages is largely a matter of society; later, in more mature life, it may be a matter of isolation. It is good for the full-grown man to withdraw at times from the city into the desert, unless perchance the city may be to him a place of solitude. There are those who are never so much alone as when the multitudes throng and press. But the fundamental idea of the school is the group. A college or seminary or university is a society, in which the conditions are favorable for rare and inspiring fellowships. Great social and moral movements have their frequent origin in these inner groups. Oxford alone has given the Wesleys and their friends, Newman and Keble and Pusey, and Arnold Toynbee and his fellow workers. Paul lays great stress, you will recall, upon the quality of like-mindedness. The group is organized around this quality. It signifies more than a common disposition or taste or liking. It carries with it oneness of aim and purpose and consecration. The group guarantees the steady impulse and the resolute endeavor. One member may lose heart: he has the common faith to fall back upon. There are times when the individual may have an immense deal to give, there are times when he needs to make great drafts upon the general fund.

We are coming to recognize the economy of the group in the more exhausting forms of moral and religious work. Service in the midst of depressing surroundings must itself be characterized by good cheer and steady courage. The constant strain upon the sympathies is the test of the real significance of living and working under wrong social conditions. I doubt if one person can well bear the strain. It is the group which saves the individual to his work, and supplies that fund of good cheer which is indispensable to spiritual success. The social settlement is founded in the idea of the spiritual economy of the group.

The settlement has already produced some very striking results, but it is contributing a principle which, as fast as it may be applied, will reinvigorate and gladden all lowlier forms of service, wherever the idea is practicable. I wish that it could be made more practicable among those entering the ministry. What it requires on their part is the willingness to postpone "a call to a church," to delay the home, and to give the first years of one's trained life to associated work in city or country. It is difficult to say where the need is the greater. The principle is equally applicable to the congested wards of a city and to the sparser settlements of the country. I am confident that a term of service in a well-organized and well-manned group will give one an impulse throughout the after ministry for which there is no equivalent.

I refer to one other influence, which reaches within the period of education and is really a part of it, whether we formally recognize it or not, namely, the interest which attaches to the moral movements of one's time. This interest may often seem to be too absorbing for the best intellectual discipline, but it cannot be, and ought not to be, ignored. The educated man cannot afford to separate himself from any movement which is to affect in vital ways his own future, or the future of those with whom he may have to do.

The American church has passed through two great moral awakenings, and is now passing through a third. What if the young men of their generation had not heard that first personal call to modern missions! Suppose the now memorable and well-nigh accomplished word of Mills to his comrades — "We ought to carry the gospel to dark and heathen lands, and we can do it if we will" — had passed through the churches unheeded; can any one calculate what the state of religion would have been in that generation, or even in this? Or can any one measure the possible moral result of a like denial of the anti-slavery conflict? The initiative in this conflict can hardly be credited to young men. Neither can it be said that the conflict was assured till "Uncle Tom's Cabin" was read in the homes, and the speeches of Seward and Sumner and Lincoln were read in the schools and colleges of the land. The present movement in behalf of social righteousness waits in like manner full recognition from the young men of the country, especially from those in the process of education; for the movement calls for insight and sagacity, as well as for consecration. The man who helps here must be both trained and consecrated, and training and consecration rest alike upon the interest which can be awakened. I commend to you, in your immediate outlook upon the ministry, the utterance of Lyman Beecher in his forecast of his own times: " I read the signs of the times. I felt as if the conversion of the world to Christ was near. It was with such views of the future that from the beginning I consecrated myself to Christ with special reference to the scenes which I saw to be opening upon the world. I have never laid out great plans. I have always waited, and watched the fulfillment of prophecy, and followed the leadings of Providence. From the beginning my mind has taken in the church of God, my country, and the world as given to Christ. It is this which has widened the scope of my activity beyond the common sphere of pastoral labor."

How far can we educate the preacher? We cannot guarantee the individual man. Out of any given number in training for the pulpit, one or more will quite surely fail to become preachers, though failure will not always follow the prediction. But the process will go on to its large results. Education, especially the education which opens into the ministry, is an ideal world, in which one learns to live till he becomes in some sense superior to the world of tradition and circumstance and struggle which lies before him. It has its own discipline, always severe and exacting. It allows no interferences with its aims and standards. But it is not narrow or artificial. It offers the inspiration of the master, it introduces the stimulus of the group, and it stands open to the moral enthusiasm of the age. It is a world by no means free from doubts or temptations. Not all is gain to those within it. Much power has to be expended in resistance to dangerous forces which inhere in its very life. But it is a world of great incentives, of stirring fellowships, and of honorable ambitions. It cannot deliver the preacher, but it can present the scholar furnished for his task, and the man made ready and expectant.

III

THE UNMAKING PROCESS

THE subject of to-day will carry us altogether within the life and work of the preacher. I am to speak of the forces and influences which stand in one way or another for his unmaking. The subject of my lecture is The Unmaking Process, if that can be called a process which may have no clear sequence of causes. What is cause at one time may be effect at another time. What is cause with one man may be effect with another man. All that we can say is that there are influences which are continually present to undermine or disintegrate or demoralize the preacher. They may be resisted. And in so far as they are resisted, the preacher has the advantage which always attends the successful defense of anything which is as sacred as preaching. I do not wish to make this lecture a chapter on the moral deterioration of ministers. It will answer its purpose if I can expose and set forth with the right emphasis some of the more subtle influences which are working to undo the preacher, or to neutralize his power.

The foe which lies in wait for the preacher from beginning to end is unreality. I do not know whether the danger is greater at the beginning or at the end, but I naturally dwell in your presence more upon the danger at the beginning. It is always difficult to be real, but never more difficult than when one tries at first to put all his newly acquired powers to use.

Preaching consists in the right correspondence between the apprehension and the expression of a given truth. The morality of preaching lies at this point, just where also its effectiveness lies. Preaching becomes unmoral, if not immoral, when the preacher allows the expression of truth to go beyond the apprehension of it. This is unreality in the pulpit. Doubtless some unreal preaching is effective, but never for long time. The law is, that the power of the pulpit corresponds to the clearness and vividness of the preacher's apprehension of truth. The preacher who really believes the half truth will have more power than the preacher who half believes the truth. But it is almost equally true that preaching may fail for want of adequate expression. Hence the occasion for the art of sermonizing, or for the art of preaching; the art, that is, of making the expression of truth satisfy the apprehension of it. This art, because it is an art, has its own moral danger. I shall speak of other phases of the art in my next lecture, but I now touch upon the moral element involved in it.

Unreality comes into preaching usually at one of these three points: First, through the commitment of a truth to some one faculty exclusively, — to the reason, or the imagination, or the emotions. Logic, as we well know, may lead us into the impossible, the unbelievable. The conclusion of the dogma of an arbitrary election in the dogma of infant damnation was logical enough, but it could not find acceptance in the category of Christian doctrine. It could never gain the consent of any other faculty than the logical faculty. Outside the sphere of logic it was reckoned impossible, unbelievable. The imagination and the emotions cannot be trusted alone any more than the reason. Things are not necessarily true because we want them to be true, nor because we can describe them as if they were true. Nothing can be more unreal than the work of the imagination when it is divorced from feeling, or when it advances in some directions beyond the power of feeling. It is for this reason, I suppose, that the descriptions of the future torment of the wicked, as given by the old preachers, are as a rule so ineffective. They are certainly no more effective than the descriptions of the dramatists. But the preacher is more closely bound to reality than the dramatist, although reality is the mark of genuineness in all literature. I emphasize the danger of intrusting truth to any one faculty. The test of reality is the consent of the whole nature. A man has no right to say, I believe, unless the whole man believes. No creed can live which is repeated under the protest of any part of the consecrated nature.

A second point at which unreality may

come into the pulpit is through undue striving after effect. The motive may be right, the preacher wants to get a hearing for the truth. When Robert Hall says that "miracles were the bell of the universe which God rang to call men to hear his Son," we see the propriety of the figure. Truth must have a hearing. But when we take unfit, exaggerated, unscrupulous methods to get a hearing for the truth, we rob it of its reality. Here is the vice of sensationalism. Truth in the hands of a sensationalist does not impress us with its reality. We discount so much that the little which is left is ineffective. It must be the same to the man himself who deals in the sensational method. He cannot take the truth seriously, in so far as he is using it for mere effect. And all like strivings for effect, whether in style of speech or manner of delivery, fall under the same charge of unreality.

And the third point at which danger comes in is through undue stimulus from an audience. Extempore preachers are often charged with rhetorical courage. They borrow their courage, the charge is, from the situation. They say things in public as they would not say them in private, if indeed they would say them at all. Rhetorical courage is not necessarily unreal courage. One may legitimately do that on an occasion which he could not do without the occasion. We must give a large liberty to public utterance. That may be perfectly real to one in the presence of men, and under the common feeling when once it is awakened, which could not be real in the same degree to one when alone. Still it is a part of the spiritual obligation of the preacher not to be dependent for the reality of great truths upon the occasional excitement. He is to be the steadier force among men. He is to make the positive, as Mr. Emerson says, stronger than the superlative. He ought to have no need of exaggeration. He must never allow himself to utter as truths any of those sentiments which cannot be verified to some degree in the common experience.

These are the dangers which threaten the preacher at the beginning. They all come from the failure to get the right correspondence between the apprehension of truth and the expression of it. I do not say that they are greater at the beginning of one's work than at the end. The young preacher may want to express too much. The older preacher may not dare to express enough. Certainly, if conservatism is the mark of age, it has its dangers. There is a saving of truth which is a losing, a fear for the truth which comes to be a distrust of it. The ultra conservatism of the pulpit which stands more and more for the defense of truth, whose chief concern is that the truth shall suffer no harm, makes the preacher himself less and less an outgoing force. He, too, becomes unreal, because he no longer comes up to the measure of the truth.

Next to the danger of the preacher from unreality, I put the danger which comes from the want of direct and wholesome criticism. Criticism of a certain sort there is in abundance, but it never reaches the preacher's ears. For aught he knows, unless he is a man of rare insight, he is exempt from criticism. Contrast his situation with that of the young advocate, who makes his plea before the jury in the presence of an alert antagonist, or even with that of the young author, who waits the word of the reviewer. The want of an open antagonist or critic is, I think, the greatest disadvantage of an intellectual sort from which the pulpit suffers.

When Mr. Webster was at Marshfield, an old friend said to him, " Mr. Webster, were you ever practically helped by anybody in forming your style?" "Yes," Mr. Webster answered at once. "Soon after I was admitted to the bar, I gave a Fourth of July oration at Portsmouth. The editor of a magazine in Philadelphia published the oration with a running comment upon it. Taking it up part by part, he said: 'This passage shows good reasoning; here is a bit of eloquence; but here is a lot of rhetoric, mere wording. If the speaker cannot learn to use simple and sincere language, he can never be the orator for the common people.' I read that criticism over and over," Mr. Webster said, "and finally concluded that if I was to get my living by talking to plain people, I must have a plain style."

How invaluable a just and competent

critic would be to a young preacher. But instead of that the average preacher has much to fear from flattering tongues. Few men are insensible to flattery. And preachers are more liable, not susceptible, to this enervating experience than any other class of men, with the possible exception of actors. I wonder at the liberties which men and women take in this regard with the preacher. They seem to assume that the preacher is a non-resistant. Appreciation is a virtue. There is none too much of it. It is not only grateful, it may be inspiring. But flattery, or mere compliment, or even unthinking acquiescence, each and all are enervating to the last degree. As far as they have an effect, they hold the preacher to his lower levels. Far better the stimulus, the spur, if need be, the goad. I count it the sure mark of deterioration when one begins to be content and satisfied with himself, because others, it matters not whether they be few or many, are apparently satisfied with him, and say so. In the absence of open criticism the preacher must learn how to interpret facts which stand for criticism. Absence is criticism;

inattention is criticism; unresponsiveness is criticism; and the failure to secure appreciable results may be criticism. The preacher is the last man who can afford to ignore or misinterpret facts which have a bearing on his personal or professional growths.

You will not be surprised when I remind you that the preacher has much to fear from the dissipation of personal energy. A very competent authority, himself enough on the inside to observe, has said that the two besetting sins of the ministry are laziness and lying. By lying he means the essential thing about which we have been talking under the name of unreality. But by laziness he means, I take it, the disposition or the willingness to do the lesser in place of the greater duty. This is the subtle refinement of laziness always and everywhere, the postponement of the hard and exacting duty beyond the one which is easier and more agreeable. The minister has an unwonted range of duties. Every day gives a large choice. He can satisfy his conscience by keeping at work indiscriminately. He can be the busiest man in town, and yet leave his great task undone. He is simply working out of proportion. *He* can do this; few other men can. And every preacher is working out of proportion when he does not make preaching the one high, commanding, inspiring duty of his life. I do not underestimate the exactions or the joys which belong to the pastorate. But I do say that the imperative obligation of the minister is to his pulpit. And when distractions multiply and duties apparently conflict, he ought to be able to hear, and to know that he must obey, the mandate of the pulpit, — "Enter into thy closet and shut thy door."

No, I do not mean this literally. I commend to you the necessity to the preacher of the power of mental abstraction. A preacher cannot altogether control time or place. He ought not to expect to do this. He must make allowance for interruptions. As Dr. Payson used to say, "The man who wants to see me is the man whom I want to see," a rule of present application, barring book agents and college presidents. The preacher who excludes himself from men in the time of their want or necessity is the preacher whose sermons will in time betray this seclusion. What, then, is the preacher's defense? The power of concentration or of abstraction, the power to hold a subject in thought and in heart under interruption or in the midst of distracting influences. A preacher ought to consider it one part of his mental training to make himself reasonably independent of conditions. He ought to be able to work on a train, if he has elbow room, not perhaps as well, but as resolutely, as in his study. He ought to be able to think clearly and calmly, or clearly and passionately, in the midst of alien surroundings, as well as when he is within reach of his favorite authors, provided of course he does not need to consult them.

And beyond this consecration of the preacher to the pulpit, I advise strongly that a preacher seek first and above all things to gain a secure standing in his own pulpit. No people have the like claim upon him with his own people; and no causes have a like claim upon him at the beginning with the cause for which his own pulpit stands. Later I shall have occasion to speak of the growing range of a preacher's activity, but at the first, a preacher has the imperative duty, which he owes alike to himself and to his people, of concentrating upon his own pulpit. I commend the example of Dr. Gordon at the opening of his pastorate at the Old South Church, Boston, who resolved that for three years he would make no public addresses. He kept his resolution. To-day he has the freedom of the country.

There is a very strong though subtle influence which is at work toward the unmaking of the preacher, coming up out of the social situation. The social situation is continually thrusting the question into the preacher's face, How much ought you to sacrifice for the people about you, most of whom are in circumstances of comfort, a few in circumstances of luxury? If he were a pioneer in a new country, or if he were a missionary among some peoples, this question would not arise. A part of the heroism of the missionary in distinction from the routine of the parish minister lies in the social sacrifice. There is evident need of that sacrifice. Hardship, privation, possibly suffering, show the price of his consecration. But why should a minister, the insidious question will surely arise, whose lot is cast in the midst of social plenty and refinement,— why should he sacrifice anything? and if he is to make no sacrifice, why should he not want and expect the many and various privileges for which society stands? The question becomes a very absorbing one when once it begins to enter seriously into the thought of a minister, or into the thought of his family. And there is no end to its perplexities. It has more power of petty distractions than all other questions put together. The Presbyterian Church seems to have settled the difficulty in the terms of the call which a local church extends to a pastor. The call runs in this wise:—

" And that you may be free from worldly cares and avocations, we hereby promise and oblige ourselves to pay to you the sum of —— in regular quarterly (or half yearly, or yearly) payments, during the time of your being and continuing the regular pastor of this church."

This seems to settle the question; but if the terms of a call are freely met, this would be far from a settlement of the difficulties of the social situation. The salaries of ministers are graduated everywhere very closely to ordinary expense. They are in this respect like the salaries of teachers and professors, or for that matter like the salaries of congressmen and judges, the salaries of any persons outside the commercial classes. But the wants of a minister and his family are the same with those of the average members of the community in which they live. Their tastes are probably rather above the average, and beyond these lies the appeal of ambition and privilege and opportunity.

What, now, can the preacher do? I say unhesitatingly he must accept in the main the social situation as it is, and find his satisfying compensations in the peculiar aims and opportunities of his work. By this I do not mean that the business side of the ministry is to be made light of. It is one of the first duties of a minister to see that a parish gives for its own uses up to the full limit of self-respect. Nothing is gained to charity, but everything is lost, by condoning with stinginess. That parish will give most to foreign missions which is trained to meet its own obligations to the full. But when this has been done, I know of nothing further to be done except for a preacher to turn himself with contentment and satisfaction to his work. He cannot work under a social grievance. He cannot preach and complain. But a great many preachers are complaining. I think that there is more complaint in the ministry than in any other profession or calling; and of the various branches of the church, I think that there is the most restlessness and complaint in the Congregational ministry. The Methodist system determines a preacher's lot and in part, at least, his disposition toward it. The Episcopal ideal supports the minister through the dignity and separateness of his position. The Congregational ministry is essentially democratic. That means that it feels the strain of social equality. The very spirit which, as I shall show you by and by, makes it difficult for us to maintain our churches in certain localities, makes it difficult to maintain our ministers in a state of mind reasonably free from social competitions and embarrassments. And therefore I apprise you in advance of the peculiar danger from this source.

Let me go a step further in the same direction and speak of the loss of power to the preacher from frequent changes. I conceive that the shortness and changeableness of the pastorate are doing a great deal at present toward the unmaking of the preacher. I know that there are two sides to this matter; and especially that it may seem to have a different aspect as one looks at it from the side of the minister or of the congregation. It is, I believe, among the traditions of this place, that when a student asked Mr. Beecher, "What was the special reason for short pastorates," he got the quick reply, "The mercy of God."

Permanency in the pastorate, other things being equal, is a tremendous source of power to the pulpit. It gives the preacher the advantage of the accumulations in his personality. The old rhetoricians used to say that one office of an introduction was to present the speaker and gain acceptance for him with his audience. The preacher, who rises in the pulpit after years of preaching, is a known man, and if known probably honored and loved. If he has shown intellectual advance, the congregation is expectant of more truth. When he applies that in hand, his wisdom in the past enforces his application. And when he appeals to his people, every influence from character and association and personal kindness and sacrifice goes with the appeal.

There is but one valid argument on the other side, speaking now in the interest of the truth, of which I am aware. It is the argument from freshness, the chance for the new truth or the new setting of it. But this all depends upon the question as to whether the preacher's past is for him or against him. If he cannot improve upon that, if he repeats himself, if he is no more to the truth than formerly, then he ought to go. But if he can keep himself abreast of truth, continually in advance of his people, and maintain the good cheer and enthusiasm of his personal faith, then he ought to stay, so far as the interests of truth are concerned.

And now about other interests, and especially about that of the preacher himself. The community, it goes without saying, is usually the loser when a man is called away under the urgent solicitation of another parish. If this were not the case, calls from one parish to another would be very scarce. But how about the minister himself? It must be true that the man who is under frequent call to leave his parish can afford to stay. At least, he need not fear lest the last opportunity has come to him. But can he satisfy the proper demand for what may be the larger field? Let him ask himself if he has enlarged his field to the utmost. Has he pushed out into all legitimate relations to other fields of work entirely germane to the preacher? One of the most popular of our younger preachers has declined a call to a large city on the ground, in part, that his influence is extending into the colleges, and that he cannot afford to forego that extension of his ministry. That fact suggests one of the new sources of pulpit power. Every board of preachers in the colleges makes ten men necessary where one served for the place a generation ago. The work of the pulpit is growing more intensive and extensive. Preaching has to be clearer and more direct, more to the point, than ever before. And it has to do with wider relations. I am very careful about advising interference with social and semi-political issues till one is thoroughly trained and prepared for such business. But this outer ministry has a place in every tried, enlarged, influential pastorate, provided the preacher shows personal aptitude. I see no need of frequent changes of pastorate, in the interest of freshness, either to preacher or people, if the preacher will use all his opportunities to keep himself in close and quickening relations to truth and men. I cannot overestimate the power to the pulpit of men whose personality has begun to count for something before the public. Usually this power comes from men who are placed. They are institutions. What matters it just where the preacher is, if when he speaks he gets the wider hearing, if the book he prints is read, if the cause he advocates is forwarded, if the inspiration of his life and work goes out from heart to heart. I am not saying that a man should stay always where he begins, though I think he ought to stay long enough to pay the people for having taught him his apprenticeship; but I am protesting against the restlessness which comes with so great frequency of change in the pastorate. Greater permanency would, I am sure, give us better churches and better preachers.

One of the chief sources of discouragement in one's early ministry is disappointment in men. This disappointment does not usually extend to loss of faith in human nature, though a tendency to generalize from a few particular cases of disappointment is very strong, and the result in such instances very disheartening. Whenever the result is suspicion, distrust, or personal bitterness, a preacher's power is greatly lessened, and sometimes utterly lost. But the danger which I now have in mind, while less, is enhanced by the fact that it comes to one early. I recall with gratitude the advice which I received as a younger man from the Hon. Alpheus Hardy, of

Boston, "Don't expect too much of men." No layman within my knowledge had higher standards than he. No man had a more scrupulous sense of honor in business or a broader sense of public obligation. But his words were wise. I have had frequent occasion to prove their meaning. Men at large are not only under greater temptations than we may suppose, but they are under greater restrictions in the matter of right doing than we may suppose. I think that the pulpit often lays a burden on the individual man which ought to be shared by society. The preacher is continually saying to the man in business or politics, or in any of the departments of worldly struggle, repent, repent. And the call is none too strong. But, on the other hand, what if the individual man replies, as he does by his silence and neglect, "How can I repent? how can I repent alone? I represent my calling, my business, my party, my sect. When you ask me to repent, you virtually ask me to leave my business or calling or party or sect. For when I have done all that I can to reform the situation of which I am a part,

I am still a party to very much which you condemn and which I disapprove."

Here lies the argument to-day, gentlemen, for the training of the social conscience. I do not say that we have no right to urge individual repentance, and works meet for repentance, but I do say that we have no right to expect the full and proper response to our message till we have made the conditions more nearly possible for personal righteousness. The call to repentance which we send out must be addressed to the church, to society, to every calling and business which ought to listen and obey. We ought to make it harder for men to sin and more possible, if not easier, for men to be righteous. Meanwhile, let us not be disappointed in men, if we can see discontent and struggle on their part. Let us incorporate every gain in personal righteousness into public sentiment. We do not need to-day mere come-outers; we need men who will help from within, men who will leave their business or profession, and society and the state and the church, safer places to live in than when they found them.

I am not intending to speak in this lecture, or at any time, about the great lapses from faith or from righteousness or from God, which completely undo the preacher. They are self-evident in their application. I speak only the passing word about the effect of intellectual doubt upon the power of the preacher. The effect of doubt depends upon the kind of doubt. There is a doubt which is utterly demoralizing. There is a doubt which is a challenge to sincere and brave souls. Who questions the effect of doubt on the soul of Robertson? What mighty and passionate sympathies it gave him with humanity. What depth of view it gave him into the heart of truth. How near it brought him to the personal Christ. Doubt of such a nature, and it is the only kind worthy of a strong and sane man, may have an incalculable power for good. It may lead the way into reality. When the darkness is spent, it is the true light which shineth.

The most serious danger to the preacher must of course come from himself. I cannot make clear all the ways in which it will become real to you. But there is one aspect of the danger which I cannot overlook, because it grows with the true growth and success of the preacher. The longer one lives, the harder one works, the better in some senses the results of his preaching, the farther apart the man seems to himself to be from the truth he utters. I do not see how it can be otherwise. Ideals must outstrip the reality. The increasing brightness of the truth brings out more clearly personal deficiencies and shortcomings. In the very joy of preaching there may come in upon one the sense of personal unworthiness which is overwhelming. The success which one may gain may seem to him to have a lower interpretation. He cannot accept the verdict of the hour. He anticipates a diviner judgment, which may be a reversal of that which has apparently been rendered. I am about to read you an extract from one of the greatest, — it is altogether the most searching sermon of the last generation, that of Canon Mozley on the Reversal of Human Judgment. I count each year in especial danger which has not felt the tonic of its words.

"Suppose any supernatural judge should appear in the world now, it is evident the scene he would create would be one to startle us; we should not soon be used to it; it would shock and appall; and that from no other cause than simply its reductions; that it presented characters stripped bare, denuded of what was irrelevant to goodness, and only with their moral substance left. The judge would take no cognizance of a rich imagination, power of language, poetical gifts, and the like, in themselves, as parts of goodness, any more than he would of richness and prosperity; and the moral residuum left would appear perhaps a bare result. The first look of divine justice would strike us as injustice; it would be too pure a justice for us; we should be long in reconciling ourselves to it. Justice would appear, like the painter's gaunt skeleton of emblematic meaning, to be stalking through the world, smiting with attenuation luxuriating forms of virtue. Forms, changed from what we knew, would meet us, strange, unaccustomed forms, and we would have to ask them who they were, — 'You were flourishing but a short while ago, what has happened to you now?' And the answer, if it spoke the truth, would be, 'Nothing, except that now much which lately counted as goodness counts as such no longer; we are tried by a new moral measure, out of which we issue different men; gifts which have figured as goodness remain as gifts, but cease to be goodness.' Thus would the large sweep made of human canonizations act like blight or volcanic fire upon some rich landscape, converting the luxury of nature into a dried-up scene of bare stems and scorched vegetation."

Sometimes I say, Yes, more and more, this sense of dissatisfaction with personal gifts, this sense of their danger as substitutes for plain and simple righteousness, finds a place in the heart of the preacher. It is perhaps as much a sign of the true spirit and of the growing reality, as the trembling knee is the inseparable sign of eloquence. The preacher has the right to know that humility is the one sure possession which gives him entrance into the high places of his high calling.

> "Humble must be if to heaven we go,
> High is the roof there, but the gate is low."

I once asked Dr. Philip Schaff to preach for me. As we passed through the doorway near the foot of the pulpit stairs, he turned to me and said, " Don't you always feel humble when you go through this door?" I knew at least that he felt what he said, and I knew that, though he was not distinctively a preacher, we should have that day great preaching, and we had it.

The safety of the preacher, the safeguard from himself, lies in the growth of humility. All God's chosen ones have had it. It is the sure and fine quality which underlies their natures. It explains their shrinkings from duty, their hesitations and reluctance. It was the ground of Moses' protest, — " Who am I that I should go in unto Pharaoh?" of Isaiah's despair, — " I am undone, because I am a man of unclean lips, and I dwell in the midst of a people of unclean lips:" of Jeremiah's shrinking, — " Ah, Lord God, I am but a child:" of the abasement and of the exaltation of Paul, — " I am the least of the apostles; I am not worthy to be called an apostle." " I can do all things through Christ which strengtheneth me."

Gentlemen, there is no fellowship so great or safe or assuring as that into which we enter through humility.

IV

THE PREACHER AND HIS ART

In a course of lectures like the present, which has to do altogether with the personality of the preacher, due account must be made of those influences coming from his work or from his surroundings, which are to his harm, influences which, if undetected and unrestrained, will soon or late reach the man himself, and take the heart out of his preaching. So we gave up the lecture of yesterday to the consideration of influences of this nature. I confess to you that it is with a sense of relief that I turn again to those constructive forces and habits in which we find the guarantee of the safety and power of the preacher.

I have, however, a misgiving about the lecture of to-day. It will take me, beyond any other lecture of the course, into the immediate province of the class room. I do not know how this can be helped; but I find no little satisfaction in remembering that if by any chance my opinions should not coincide with those of the department, no greater harm will come to you than this waste of words. I say in advance, gentlemen, that the work of the department is the essential thing, not the casual utterance of a lecturer. A special train may be generously given the right of way for a trip, but it is of very little account compared with the regular travel and traffic for which the road was built, and which support it.

The subject of to-day is the Preacher, considered as an Artist.

There is no reaction upon a preacher like that from his work. That creates a habit. In the lecture of yesterday, I spoke of the morality of preaching as consisting in the right correspondence between the apprehension of truth and the expression of it. Preaching becomes unmoral, if not immoral, when the expression of a truth is beyond the apprehension of it. Then the preacher crosses over the line into unreality. But I also said that the effectiveness of preaching lies in this same correspondence. It is just as necessary that the expression of truth should satisfy the apprehension or realization of it, as that the expression should not surpass the realization. When the attempt is made to communicate more truth than one has in actual possession, or when feeling is simulated, preaching becomes, so far as the preacher is concerned, an immorality. But this is not the danger of the majority of preachers, certainly not at the beginning. The danger then is that the preacher will not communicate the truth he has, or express the feeling which he actually entertains towards it. Hence the occasion for the art of preaching or sermonizing, the art of making the communication of truth satisfy the personal apprehension of it. In so far, therefore, as preaching is an art, the preacher is an artist, and ought to have the conscience of an artist; conscience, I say, for conscience is just as much concerned with the communication of truth as it is with the search after it. The conscience of the preacher as an inquirer or believer is never at variance with the conscience of the preacher when he is doing his work as an artist, and never demands that this work shall take a subordinate place. This is the fundamental position of the present lecture; and if any one is not prepared to accept it in full, then I cannot expect to convince him of the moral significance of the subject of to-day to the present course of lectures.

The preacher, considered as an artist, is to be judged by his use of method, by his sense of proportion, by his style, and by the tone of his preaching.

There are two, and, as it seems to me, but two, perfectly natural methods of preaching. One where the sermon is prepared for extempore speech, the other where the sermon is written to be read. Between these lie two other methods in common use, entirely legitimate, in themselves forcible, and probably best adapted to the average preacher, — the memoriter method, and that of the sermon written to be delivered. I will give a brief characterization of each method for our present uses.

The characteristic of the extempore method, as I view it, is that the mind of the preacher remains in the creative mood throughout the delivery of the sermon.

The ordinary definitions of extempore speech do not satisfy this conception, as when it is said that the "extempore speaker knows what he will say, he does not know how he will say it;" or that "the extempore preacher enters the pulpit as the writer takes his pen to write." These definitions ignore the idea of the creative energy as still active under the process of speaking. The true conception of extempore preaching is that the preacher enters the pulpit before the creative fires, the fires which kindle thought, have been put out. The preacher is still in heat when he enters the pulpit. The mind is in its most intense activity, and therefore clearest and most discriminating in its action. The sermon has been thoroughly prepared, that is, thought out, otherwise it would be an example of mere impromptu preaching; but something of the material in mind may be rejected, and other material may be added. The genuine extempore preacher does not know just how the truth will possess him as he stands before men; he does not know what his audience will have to say about it. It is this unknown element which enters into and determines the best extempore preaching. The best extempore sermons, I do not say the average of them, but the best, never could have been entirely prepared in the study. The extempore preacher who is such by clear distinction usually thinks his best thoughts in the presence of men. Without the stimulus of their presence, these thoughts would not have been conceived. They are born of the quick contact of the mind of the preacher with the mind of the audience. There is a just sense in which they belong to the audience as well as to the preacher. The extempore preacher must of course be prepared to preach without these partially extraneous aids: then we have ordinary preaching. He must be prepared to welcome and utilize them: then we have extraordinary extempore preaching.

It is hardly necessary to say that this distinction separates the extempore preacher entirely from the merely ready preacher or the fluent preacher or, according to the old parlance, the unwearied preacher. He belongs to another genus. Fluency is the greatest foe to true extempore preaching. The fluent, easy, self-satisfied talker has none of the stuff in him of which extempore preachers are made.

In the memoriter method, or that of the sermon written to be delivered, — they are alike in principle, — the preacher forecasts as far as possible the situation; he prepares his sermon with his audience before him in imagination; he thinks how he will utter the given truth in their presence; and having prepared the sermon in thought and feeling to the best of his power, he commits it, in the one case to memory, and in the other case to manuscript. The memoriter preacher has a considerable advantage in ready contact with his audience, in the use of eye and gesture; the preacher from manuscript may have the advantage of using his manuscript as an instrument, an instrument of great accuracy and precision. A preacher from manuscript should never be ashamed of his manuscript. He should make his audience feel that it is a source of power, that it is an effective instrument in his hands. Preaching from manuscript, it is to be remembered, is in itself an art. As Dr. William M. Taylor has said, in speaking of the change in his own case from the memoriter method, "One must educate himself to the free and unfettered use of the full manuscript." But both the manuscript sermon and the sermon written to be delivered are in their intention oratorical. The preacher is the orator, so far as he may be, in his study; he tries to put his feeling as well as his thought into the care of his memory or of his manuscript, and then to recover them in the presence of his audience, a fact which explains clearly enough, I think, what I meant when I said that either method, though extremely forcible in itself, is by comparison with the extempore method unnatural. The aim being oratorical, the method is not so true to the aim.

The sermon written to be read is by distinction literary. It is not written to be delivered, it is written to be read. The action is not in the man speaking as the orator, the action is in the style. The style is terse, vivid, axiomatic, picturesque, vital in word as well as in thought, and everywhere pervaded by the imagination. Mere smoothness of diction is as fatal to this method as is fluency to the extempore method. Every sentence has its own carrying power. Gesture may be used, but it helps very little. The use of the eye is not necessary. I heard a preacher some twenty years ago, a young man then, now unhappily no longer in the pulpit, read a sermon of this type without lifting his eyes from the manuscript, but I doubt if any one in the large audience took his eyes off the preacher. This method, though not absolutely natural, is relatively natural. It is true to its aim. Its aim is the best expression of a truth through the most effective literary qualities. The literary aim allows the literary method of presentation, that is, reading.

Now while these methods differ, as I conceive, at the points I have named, they all have the great and essential qualities of the sermon in common. A sermon must be a sermon in any and all conceivable circumstances, as a plea must be a plea, or an essay an essay, or a poem a poem. But in the choice of a method, and in the adaptation of it to his own powers, the preacher is the artist. There lies a considerable part of the responsibility in relation to any art. And the choice is not to be quickly settled. For this reason I would advise the method of the sermon written to be delivered to begin with, as the one which secures the best immediate results, and from which one can pass into the method of the extempore or written sermon, should one feel that he is capable of making the change. The memoriter method, if one has a reliable memory, has the advantage of direct approach to an audience. The danger of the method is declamation, than which nothing can be more out of place in the pulpit.

But if one is to become the extempore preacher, or the preacher of the sermon written to be read, he must enter into long and resolute training; especially in case of training for extempore preaching, he must put himself under inexorable safeguards against uncertainty in thought, unevenness in temperament, diffuseness in language, — the fluent man, I repeat, should never become the extempore preacher, — against repetition and monotony in the choice of subjects, the overworking of words and phrases, overstatement, undue familiarity with an audience, and various other dangers of like nature too many to be enumerated. He must subject himself to a training which is positive and continuous; and when he has his method well in hand, then he will beware most lest through overconfidence he lets in some of the vices which will destroy its power. But the end, as indeed the end to be reached by any method, is worthy of the struggle. Just so far as conscience goes into the task, just so far may one take to himself the joy of his conscience in the result.

Proportion in the sermon reveals the artist in the preacher more even than his use of method. A sermon proceeding upon any method must have proportion. It is the artistic test. I once heard a sermon from a very able man on the hidings of God's power. These hidings, the preacher said, were to be found in history, in providence, and in grace. It took the preacher thirty minutes to find them in history, ten minutes to find them in providence, and three minutes to find them in grace. The element of time, considering the sermon as a whole, enters into the question of proportion. A preacher must determine how long a given truth, under his presentation of it, can hold an audience for the best impression, not how long an audience will stay and return another Sunday. The arrangement of a sermon has a great deal to do with the impression of time. Some preachers frighten an audience at the outset by the way in which they lay out a sermon, even when the fear is not justified by the actual time taken. I have in mind a preacher who lays out his sermon for an hour, but he always stops inside thirty minutes. I suppose it may have been a man of this type who raised in the mind of Sydney Smith the horrible suspicion, which he communicated to his neighbor in the pew — "You don't suppose, do you, that the man has forgotten the end?"

Proportion demands of the preacher that he shall always choose a manageable subject, and this means sometimes that he shall leave a subject alone, it may be for years, until it becomes manageable. A manageable subject is one which can be presented in its wholeness. Wholeness requires unity, but it is more than unity.

It is bringing the weight of the subject to bear, not in fragments, but as a whole. Proportion calls for emphasis in the distinction of parts. Equality of treatment measured in time and space may be a false equality. One part may be made emphatic by the simple statement of it; another part requires full and elaborate treatment. Proportion is not a matter of outline. It is a matter of impression. When a thought has done its work, then the next. Or to change from the figure of structure, which always restricts the thought of proportion, let me say that the characteristic of a sermon from beginning to end is movement, progress. You can test the sermon at any point by this characteristic. There is no such thing, for example, as the introduction to a subject. Introduction is a part of the subject. It is that part which invites entrance. Once within, the mind is carried along by the preacher, now by argument, now by illustration, now by appeal, but always carried along. At any given moment the listener is not where he was the moment before. And when the end comes, one knows that he has been under motion. A sermon that has had movement cannot stop without creating this feeling in an audience, even if it has not been apparent before. The stillness which has prevailed gives way to the movement of relief. The tension is broken.

Under whatever figure you consider the idea of proportion, it comes to the same thing. The preacher has given the right amount of truth for the end sought, he has kept its unity, he has left it with an impression which does justice to the truth as a whole. And meanwhile the appropriate effect is to be seen in the audience. The audience is brought to a conclusion, not the sermon simply, or the truth. " Preaching," according to one of the best definitions of it of which I have knowledge, " is making men think, and feel as they think, and act as they feel."

The pulpit, as much as any agency of public speech, places insistence upon style. The truth in itself, however true it may be, will not insure the preacher a hearing. It is in preaching as in all good speech, the truth, plus the man, plus the style. The pulpit, however, insists upon no particular style. It has no style of its own. The attempt to create something distinctive and peculiar in this regard always results in unnaturalness, the worst possible vice in preaching. What the pulpit demands, and all that it demands, is adherence to the fundamental laws of effective speech. It continually throws the emphasis upon the most elementary and fundamental qualities. There must be vitality, the one physical quality, the expression of which may vary from the restraint of the deep, almost impossible utterance to the outburst of passion, but the quality must be in evidence. The preacher must be alive, the sermon must be a living thing, otherwise the inference will be against the truth as well as against the preacher. And there must be sincerity, the one moral quality; sincerity in the choice of a subject and at every step in its presentation; a sincerity so absolute that it will insure the denial of all ambitious themes, the rejection of all unproven or unreal statements, the contempt of all feigned emotion; a sincerity also which will show itself in the quickening of the whole moral nature and in its ready and complete response to the truth.

The literary qualities of the sermon which are in demand are equally clear and simple. I would lay the stress upon these three, — plainness, force, and beauty.

What is necessary to insure plainness in the sermon? First, that the thought of the sermon be prepared for others. The thinking of the preacher is not to take the place of the thinking of the audience, but it is to adapt itself to their thought to the degree that it may prove a stimulus. There must be no strangeness, no remoteness in the thought of the pulpit. It must not be alien to the current life of men. What are called "living subjects" are not necessarily subjects of the hour, but subjects through which life is always flowing in steady current. The preacher must learn to think toward men, not away from them. Why should he not learn to think in their terms, just as he always shares the common feeling? There is no more reason for the divorce of the pulpit from the intellectual life of the people than there is for its divorce from their emotional life. And second, that the sermon have order of thought. Order is the chief aid to understanding. A sermon should be so arranged or developed that a hearer can never lose his place in it. The preacher can count upon a good deal of simple logic in the common mind. There may not be enough to expose sophistry, but there is always enough to follow clear reasoning on plain matters. And third, that the sermon have simple construction, or movement in its parts. A clear thought may be utterly lost in a complicated sentence. An involved period may cost the preacher the attention of his audience. Conciseness may sometimes be carried to the point of obscurity, but conciseness never leads the mind astray. Conciseness will not tolerate a wandering mind. And fourth, that the words employed in the sermon be the words of well understood and accepted speech. They must be current words. Some preachers need to take their ideas to the exchangers. They will not always receive in return short, homely words. A term of Latin derivation may be more common than its corresponding Saxon form. Familiarity is the chief test. Still, the preference goes with the strong, sinewy, terse word rather than with the more elegant or even more scrupulously exact word. I commend to you the advice which Charles Kingsley puts into the mouth of the wife of the country esquire of Harthover House: "So she made Sir John write to the 'Times' to command the Chancellor of the Exchequer for the time being to put a tax on long words: a light tax on words of over three syllables, which are necessary evils, like rats, but which like them must be kept down judiciously; a heavy tax on words of over four syllables, such as heterodoxy, spontaneity, spuriosity, and the like; and on words of over five syllables a totally prohibitory tax, and a similar prohibitory tax on words derived from three or more languages at the same time." Plainness depends upon such simple requisites as these which I have named; but it rises to finer issues, as in the power to simplify, the gift of the great teachers; or in the power to make vivid, the gift of those who have imagination as well as reason.

The quality of force is illustrated by different types of personality. Its expression is determined largely by the temperament of the speaker. There are two distinct classes of speakers who may be rightly termed forcible. In the one class power lies in repose, in the other it is in strong, intense, it may be, vehement action. The one class holds an audience, taking command of it by authority. The other class projects itself upon an audience, and arouses, inspires, or inflames. Not many speakers are able to contradict the conditions of persuasive speech, and produce results in others which are not manifest in themselves. In this regard Mr. Phillips was the exceptional orator of our generation, the only man within sound of his own words who could remain cool and unimpassioned. The distinction which I have drawn between force in comparative repose and force in personal action is quickly recognized in the distinction between Edwards and Chalmers, Webster and Choate, Finney and Moody, Conkling and Blaine, Spurgeon and Brooks. The versatility of Mr. Beecher enabled him to cover both types, though his usual type was that of the impassioned speaker. I recall with great vividness of impression one example of the range of his eloquence. It was upon the occasion of the reception of English delegates at the first National Congregational Council, held in Boston, near the close of the civil war. The state of feeling between England and the United States was then very different from that which we are now witnessing. It was no easy task for the English delegates to present the greetings of the English churches. But the men themselves were not at their best. Their words were not well chosen. The audience as it listened grew more excited and aroused. When Mr. Beecher, who had just returned from his triumphant tour in England, rose to reply — it was a personal, not an official reply — he faced a vast body of men in the heat of smothered passion. His opening words met the mood of the audience. "When I landed in England and first met the people," he said, " it seemed to me that God had sent them a strong delusion, that they should believe a lie, that they all might be damned." Then, with inimitable humor and pathos, as he described the scenes of his campaign, he relieved the tension and unburdened the heart of his hearers. And then having made his audience plastic to his touch, he began to mould it to his end. His speech broadened, as it advanced, to the limits of Christian charity, and rose to the height of moral passion befitting the subject and the occasion. It was the speech of a man who had himself in perfect command as well as his argument, and who was therefore able to command his audience. He found his audience restless and angered; he left it calmed and elevated, at peace with itself, if not altogether at peace with the outer world.

If one may attempt to describe force by its qualities rather than by the personal expression of it, I should say that it consisted in such qualities as these: directness, the power of straightforward, onmoving speech, speech which brooks no interruption but which moves with a steadfast determination to its end, not the mere advance of logic, but the advance of the whole man; copiousness, the utterance of the full man, which relieves at once the fear of mental exhaustion and gives the assurance of power in reserve; nervousness of style, the characteristic of which is that every thought is alive, that every word leaps to its task; and massiveness, the weight of well-organized thought, through which the speaker is able to make the whole of his thought felt through every part.

I do not dare to venture upon any definition of beauty, in its application to style, within the limit of a paragraph. Certainly beauty does not consist in faultlessness nor in any rhetorical devices. It is chiefly the product of the imagination, the sane imagination. It attends greatness of thought, not its mere refinements. It belongs to the positive, the real, the spiritual. It is to be found in such simplicity of conception as marked Mr. Lincoln's Gettysburg Address, in Ruskin's appreciation of nature, in Shakespeare's insight and perfection of form.

These are the qualities of style, upon which I would insist, for the pulpit. I cannot conceive of a good sermon which does not show vitality and sincerity, which is not plain and forceful, and in which the trained mind at least may not feel at some point the presence of beauty.

To speak of the tone of the sermon as belonging to its artistic side may seem to be going beyond the range of art, but I think not. Tone is personal, it belongs to the man, but it belongs to the preacher as such in his relation to given conditions and to a well-defined occasion. The pulpit tone has become a term of cant. Let us remember that the counterfeit assumes the genuine, the caricature, the original. The language of the pulpit must be the language of certainty; that gives character to its speech. It must be the language of sympathy; that gives character to its speech. It must be the language of hopefulness, the hopefulness of the gospel; that gives character to its speech. Its speech must be characterized by that spiritual quality which is no more satisfied with mere intellectualism than with sensuousness. The sermon is the utterance of a man who feels in all his nature his dependence upon God, who stands in awe of the divine working in and through him, but who rejoices none the less in the joy of the divine fellowship. Can anything declare in a more perfect simplicity the secret of the inner life of the preacher than the opening words of the Apostle John in his first epistle? " That which was from the beginning, that which we have heard, that which we have seen with our eyes, that which we beheld, and our hands handled, concerning the Word of life (for the life was manifested, and we have seen, and bear witness, and declare unto you the life, the eternal life, which was with the Father, and was manifested unto us); that which we have seen and heard declare we unto you also, that ye also may have fellowship with us: yea, and our fellowship is with the Father, and with his Son Jesus Christ: and these things we write, that our joy may be fulfilled."

Yes, the sermon ought to have a character which befits it. That gives it tone. But character in speech can come only out of the life of the speaker. If it be true in any sense that "the style is the man," it is tenfold more true that the tone is the man. And yet I am well aware of the common fact that the best men are not always the best preachers; nor is the fact to be overlooked, that the best preachers, who have the fine distinction of character in their speech, often preach below their subject and below themselves. I will not attempt any full explanation of this falling short of the pulpit in its best estate. I will, however, suggest one reason why, as it seems to me, the pulpit in any given case may lack the right tone. The lack may be due to a certain want of timeliness in the immediate preparation for preaching. The intellectual and the emotional have not been made to act in close and continuous companionship. As a result, when the time comes to preach, the intellectual element is found to be immature, or the emotional element has become a spent force. To be able to utter a truth in heat, and yet when it has taken form and shape, and reached its great conclusion — that is preaching. But what preacher has not felt the fires burning low or dying out under the process of elaboration? The truth wrought out at last is not the truth which first laid hold upon the heart and cried out for utterance. The greater experiences of the preacher are the reverse of this, when the truth grows warmer as it grows clearer, when it flames as it expands, and finally comes forth not only radiant in its own light, but touched with emotion. Touched with emotion, this is often the touch which makes the old new and the common fresh. As a quaint old commentator said, after reading Paul's words to the Philippians, — " I have told you often, and now I tell you *weeping*," — " Ah, Paul, that makes it a new truth. You have not said just that before."

V

WHAT THE PREACHER OWES TO THE TRUTH

In the lectures of this week I shall endeavor to show you how the making or unmaking of the preacher is determined by the way in which he meets two of his imperative responsibilities, his responsibility to the truth and his responsibility to men.

The nearest obligation of the preacher, an obligation of the nature of a discipline or of a task, is that which he owes to his art. Day by day, in season and out of season, he is at work under the increasing force of the homiletic habit. The preacher, as we saw at the last lecture, is the artist. He must have therefore the conscience of the artist. Let not a preacher imagine for a moment that he can satisfy his high calling by any kind of general or specific righteousness, if he neglect his business, his art. If God has called him to preach, He has called him to be a preacher. Preaching is more than sermonizing, more, that is, than the preparation, or the writing, or the delivering of a sermon. It involves the constant study of all the conditions which make the sermon effective. If a sermon is ineffective, the preacher has no right to go on making sermons just like it. He must stop and ask why it is ineffective, and not be content until he has found out the reason. That is the way in which any other man works, who has put himself under moral obligation to his art.

But quite beyond any obligation of this nature, and in a sense quite above it, are those responsibilities which a preacher assumes toward the truth and toward men. And in the treatment of these responsibilities we may find the clearest evidence of the tendencies which are at work for the making or the unmaking of the individual preacher.

The subject of to-day is The Responsibility of the Preacher to the Truth, with special reference to present conditions.

The preacher, in distinction from other men who are concerned with the truth, has a threefold responsibility: First, that the truth shall have a hearing. Second, that it shall be rightly interpreted to the popular mind. Third, that it shall reach men through the proper and sufficient motive.

The first responsibility of the preacher is to gain a hearing for the truth. William Lloyd Garrison announced his personal platform as a reformer in these words: " I will not equivocate, I will not compromise, I will not retreat a single inch, and I will be heard." I believe, gentlemen, that the preacher of to-day must have something of the personal determination of the reformer. The outward situation is not one of hostility and antagonism. Apparently the preacher has the advantage of all other men in the setting of his task. Who but he has one day in seven given him for an opportunity? Who but he has an institution widespread and universally recognized standing for his support? Yet, as we well know, neither Sunday nor the church can guarantee the preacher a hearing for the truth at all commensurate with its significance or with his obligation to it.

Dr. Fisher has reminded me of the old-time custom in New Haven that whenever a preacher of repute arrived unexpectedly in the town on a week day, the church bell was rung for an evening service, which was sure to gather up the greater part of the community. Religion as an intellectual pursuit was the prevailing interest, a state of affairs which no longer exists, so far as we know, outside the parish of Drumtochty, or possibly the neighboring parish of Tilbiedrum. In our impatience, we may charge the difference to the secularization of the age. That may or may not explain the change. Certainly it does not offer the sufficient excuse; for we are bound to believe that religion has its interests, apart from any peculiar type of intellectualism which it may develop, and equal to the passing concerns of an age.

In an after-dinner speech, Justice Holmes, of the Massachusetts Supreme Court, quoted the remark of a friend to the effect that, "After all, the only interesting thing is religion;" and then added for himself, "I think it is true, if you take the word a little broadly, and include under it the passionate curiosity as well as the passionate awe which we feel in face of the mystery of the universe. This curiosity is the most human appetite in man." Now, if to this most human appetite we have, which though latent in many is constant in all, you add the incitement of great disturbing questions, questions of authority and destiny and human welfare: if you stimulate religion on the intellectual side by critical inquiry, and on the sympathetic side by contact with misery; if you call upon Christianity as an historical religion to verify its history, and as a religion of humanity to humanize the forces which control life; if, I say, you increase and stimulate the common religious instinct or appetite by these extraordinary incitements and demands, you have brought about in general the exact state of religious thought and life which now exists. Without a doubt religion is to-day, not only by its own personal rights, but in its relation to the age, a "most interesting thing."

This, of course, is a generalization in regard to the personal appeal of truth. When you break up the generalization, and reduce the subject to its commonplace conditions, when you ask how men feel about religious truth in a given locality, you are met, I grant, by comparative indifference where you might have expected interest. Church going is conceded to be less the custom than it was several generations ago; though this fact is not to be stated alone. It is also true that the proportion of church members to the whole population has increased, and that the worth of the church to the community, when measured by its benevolences and general activities, has also increased. Church going, too, is something which cannot be determined by the presence or absence of distracting influences. The church of the city is on the whole better attended than the church of the remote country; which shows that religion can contend better against strong competitions than against stagnation or lethargy. The traditions of a locality or of a sect have much to do with church going. A community is usually in whole or in part set toward the church or away from it. A preacher finds, wherever he goes, that he has an inheritance of interest or of indifference. But when the proper allowance has been made for the influences which can be counted upon to gain the truth a hearing, it still remains that a large added obligation rests upon the preacher. To satisfy this obligation he must make all legitimate use of his personality, both within and without the pulpit. There are very few uses of one's personality, which are genuine and natural, which are not legitimate. All affectation and artificiality are ruled out, all tricks and mannerisms, all imitations of other preachers, all perversion of one's own powers. But every really natural gift has a place in the pulpit. It is impossible to discuss the question of the introduction of humor into the pulpit, apart from the knowledge of the man. The humor of one preacher may be as reverent as the solemnity of another. That charming quality of quaintness, which gives the truth the constant advantage of freshness and delicate surprise and unsuspected meaning, how much more effective it is than any rhetorical elaboration or any straining after originality. And the use of dramatic power, if the power is absolutely genuine and irresistible, how surely it lays hold upon us all without respect to persons. When Father Taylor drew to his sailor chapel, where he kept the body of the house reserved for his sailors, Dr. Channing and Daniel Webster, and later John A. Andrew and his friends, it was " the touch of nature which makes the whole world kin."

I know of no limit which we can put upon the freedom of a greatly gifted man, whom God has set in the pulpit. Great gifts, however, have a various result. They may repel as well as invite. It is for this reason that the most popular preachers are seldom universally popular. They all have their limitations. Test the fact by the attempt to exchange the audiences which different men may have gathered, and I think that you would be surprised at the result. Who supposes that Canon Liddon could have retained Mr. Spurgeon's audience had it been transferred to St. Paul's, or that Mr. Spurgeon could have retained Canon Liddon's audience had it been transferred to the Tabernacle? Or apply the same test to men of such wide humanity in common as Phillips

Brooks and Dwight Moody. When Mr. Moody was in Boston some years ago, Mr. Brooks took his service at one session. After reading his sermon, which was reported in the papers, I wondered how long the same audience would have been held under that type of preaching. An audience there would have been, but not, I believe, for any long time the same.

As the element of genuine personality in the pulpit is increased it will insure an enlarged hearing for the truth, but how it will act in a given case cannot be predicated in advance. We must deal in total results. The law is, the greater the personality of the preacher, the larger the use of his personality, the wider and deeper the response of men to the truth. And the same law applies, though in less degree, to the use of personality outside the pulpit. The pastoral gift serves the truth. The preacher who can establish right relations with men at large in any community, impressing them with his genuineness, earnestness, and disinterested zeal in their behalf, has won a clientage for the truth which he holds. I will not touch upon what I may wish to say later about the knowledge of human nature in the concrete as the pastorate opens it to the preacher, but I cannot refrain from saying at this point that pastoral service is the proper apprenticeship to the pulpit. At some time the preacher ought to know human life in its details.

The preacher is not limited in the use of his personality in gaining a hearing for the truth; he has the liberty of wise invention. There is an old term, now out of use but very significant, the means of grace; means of grace are usually means of spiritual impression. It is to be remembered that the various denominations are founded upon the use of means. The Christian communions are not so clearly or widely separated from one another by doctrine or by polity as by method. As the emphasis is laid upon authority, as with the Romanist, or upon creed, as with the Presbyterian, or upon worship, as with the Episcopalian, or upon experience, as with the Methodist, you have in the main the distinguishing characteristic. Anything which is so fundamental as method must be capable of very great and extended use. Why should not the preacher use it according to his ability and according to his sense of the fitness of things? A great deal is sometimes gained by the appeal to the unused side of the spiritual nature. I noticed some years ago in a series of meetings held by Mr. Moody, in New York, that many of the most earnest attendants and supporters were Episcopalians and Quakers. The Puritan churches have made their uninterrupted appeal for many generations to the reason and conscience. Why should they not also make the appeal more distinctly and impressively to the instinct of reverence and to the craving for worship? Why should they not also carry the appeal straight to the heart? And if there be other methods which recognize and utilize any of the primary instincts of human nature, let them be brought into service. One such is the instinct for association, which underlies the various organizations, societies, and clubs, which make an opportunity for the truth. If men who would not otherwise support or even attend a service of the church will become actively interested in the church by forming a club for the maintenance of a special service, why should not the principle be recognized and the aid accepted?

I will go a step further and plead for the recognition of peculiar means, which must be limited in their use to those whose chief reliance is upon the employment of them. My illustration shall be the use of authority as exemplified by the methods of the Salvation Army. The outfit of uniform, drums, and the like is simply an outfit. The underlying principle is authority. The man who is reached by the army is asked to surrender himself absolutely to its discipline. It is assumed, in the majority of cases, that his will has been weakened. The army offers him its will, organized and disciplined, as a substitute for his own, till he is strong enough to act for himself, and in turn to contribute to the common stock. His first and constant act is obedience. He is put under orders, tasks are assigned to him, days of special denial are appointed; he is made to live under the common eye; the surrender is in every way complete, till he is transformed from a mere dependent upon others to a helper and strengthener of others. This is the philosophy of the means of grace employed by the Salvation Army, an example of the use of authority unequaled outside the Romish Church.

Certainly the question will arise how far the incidents attending the use of any great principle are to be approved or allowed. Religion can bear a good deal, but it stops short of the grotesque. As Dr. Howard Crosby once said, " If the gospel were preached by an orang-outang, it would not be the gospel." There must be some fitness between means and end. But I think that we have less to fear from unfit methods than from the lack of an aggressive invention. I believe that the church suffers more from the under-use than from the over-use of means.

I can refer only to the use by the preacher of special and applied truths to get a hearing for the essential truth. Let me say that I believe so fully in the unity of truth that I think we can afford to meet men at all points of their personal interest, provided their interests are not hobbies. Concerning the man with a hobby nothing is to be said but " to avoid him, pass not by him, turn from him and flee away." But there are outlying questions which are fairly upon the territory held by the gospel. The concerns of Christianity are wide and sensitive, and of an infinite variety. The preacher, if he has the spiritual ability, can fitly go out to men who are living in the remote regions of the Christian faith or the Christian interest, and try to bring them back with him to the heart of Christ. I am aware of the dangers of this method. The untrained preacher will fail utterly as a specialist. And the trained preacher may go too far afield in the search after the exceptional man. Still, there is an opportunity within the range of so-called special questions for introducing men's thoughts to the more personal claims of Christianity.

The second responsibility of the preacher to the truth is that of rightly interpreting it to the popular mind. The interpretation of religious truth involves the understanding of the mind to be reached as well as of the truth to be declared. A preacher may have a clear and right understanding of religious truth, but he will still fail in the interpretation of it if he does not know and estimate the state of mind before him. We can see that no amount of biblical or theological or homiletic training could enable one to interpret Christianity to the Oriental thought. The missionary must not only learn the language of an Oriental people, he must learn the thought of the people, before he can reach them to any extent. This is an extreme illustration. But we are apt, I think, to overestimate the accessibility of religious truth to the average mind of Christendom. Let us analyze the situation.

A great many people are still alien to Christian thinking who are not alien to the Christian spirit. Interpretation means in such cases the introduction of the terms of Christianity. Ask the average young person who is about to join the church, " What do you think it is to be a Christian? " or " What does it mean to you to be a Christian? " and the chances are that you will receive from one out of five an answer in general moral or religious terms. To be a Christian means to try to do right, or to attend church, or to be kind and helpful, — very good answers, but not answers lying at the heart of Christianity. Personal Christianity remains to be interpreted to such an one. The relation of the soul to Christ is to be brought out with a simplicity corresponding to the outward duty which may already exist. A great deal of the work of the pulpit, in every community, consists in making connection between Christianity and the general moral sense of people, vitalizing their existing life, purifying it, opening it out into the Christian opportunity, and giving it the motive and power which come only from the indwelling Christ.

And then there is the relation of the pulpit to a considerable amount of prejudiced mind, in the church and out of it. I suppose that there is no type of mind so unmanageable, so impervious to the advance of religious truth, as the traditionalized mind. Sometimes it finds its way into the pulpit. I once heard a minister say at his examination, as his final answer to all questions bearing upon modern inquiry, "My mother's theology is good enough for me." Doubtless his mother's religion was good enough for him or for anybody else; but when one plants himself upon his mother's theological standing, he announces that he has no use for further theological inquiry.

There is no little amount of mind of this character in and out of the church, — quite as much without as within, and, if anything, more difficult to reach. What can the preacher do with it? It is of no use to attack a prejudiced mind. You cannot always tell a man what you think of his opinions if you want to reach the man. Suppose one tells you that he believes in the inerrancy of Scripture as based on the correctness of the original autographs. I do not know of anything to do except to change the subject. You can hardly express yourself about that opinion and have a chance for further effort after the man. I do not know of the way of arguing with a literalist of any sort, with a view of convincement. The only approach to such a mind is through interpretation. You have the opportunity, Sunday after Sunday, of so opening the Scriptures in their spirit that the final result may be a deliverance from the bondage of the letter. Certainly argument is useless and controversy is wicked; there is no power outside the right use of interpretation. The spiritual must always have time in which to do its work. Familiarity with the broader truth will in time displace the narrower view.

And then there is the over-familiarized mind, both in the church and without, the mind which knows it all, which is impatient of instruction and resentful of any intimation of the need of further knowledge. This is on the whole the most common type and the most difficult to reach. It is mind which all unconsciously to itself has fallen into the commonplace. And yet you cannot say just that, you cannot accuse it of ignorance and dullness. Nothing again remains but the art of interpretation. That is enough. There lies the power to stimulate, to quicken, to awaken. Sometimes the confession will follow preaching of this order, the "whereas

I was blind, now I see;" but more frequently the preacher must be content with the gradual opening of the mental vision, and the gradual awakening of the spiritual nature.

These all represent types or states of mind to be changed, — the mind alien to Christian thought, the prejudiced mind, and the mind which has been over-familiarized with religious truth.

But the great body of mind which is before the preacher does not need to be changed. It is serious, intelligent, well-disposed, and open. What are the preacher's obligations to this prevailing class of mind? One obligation is of the time, one is permanent. The immediate obligation is to present all necessary changes in religious thought without prejudice to the religious life. It cannot be denied that we all love to believe in the unchangeableness of religion. So much is unchangeable in principle that we like to carry over this quality into things which are incidental. The traditionalist, the literalist, the ecclesiastic, have the advantage in being able to relate everything, which they believe to be or wish to make permanent, to something which is permanent. But when, as in our time, it seems necessary, to all who believe in progress, to effect changes in the outward and incidental to save the really permanent, the problem is, how to bring about these changes with the least disturbance to the life and work of the church. The most difficult manœuvre in war is change of front in battle. The manœuvre may be well executed; but if the battle be lost, the greater has failed before the less. Whatever theological changes are yet to be made in our time ought to be made without loss to the fight. This particular obligation rests almost entirely with the pulpit. The preacher is in command where truth is in conflict with all error which is of the nature of unrighteousness. He cannot forget that the main object is the victory. Neither can he overlook his obligation to the truth, as it becomes to his mind more clearly the truth. He will not be disloyal to his knowledge any more than to his convictions, but he will so interpret the truth as he sees it that the change will be constructive and not destructive. He will wait till he gets possession of the new truth positively. He will wait till he knows where to place the emphasis. He will wait till he knows how to make the right adjustment. In a word, he will interpret the truth so that it will fit the new duties which have really been in waiting for it. For you may be assured, gentlemen, that if God has brought any new truth to this age, it is to accomplish new tasks. Revelation and Providence are always so timed that truth never stands idle in the marketplace.

But the personal obligation of the preacher is always that of the larger and nobler interpretation of the truth. I know of no greater joy to the preacher than to stand with his truth, the truth with which he is aglow, before the hospitable mind. And, as compared with all other types and conditions, this is by far the largest. A preacher has nothing to fear, but everything to expect, who enters his pulpit with the deeper and fuller interpretation of familiar truth. The opening of Scripture as the result of study and insight, and I may add of personal experience, is grateful to an audience. The reward to the preacher is the growth of his people in and through the truth. He leaves them larger than when he found them. The congregation will probably have increased in numbers; it will certainly be larger by every other measurement. It will have the great dimensions, length, breadth, height, and depth.

I think that I have reserved enough time in this lecture to say what is really the essential thing, though being the essential thing it may take the less time to say it. The third and most serious obligation of the preacher to the truth is, to see that it reaches men at his hands through the sufficient and proper motive. Motive, in that lies the power of religious truth. Indirectly, incidentally, all truth may have motive. But in religious truth the motive gives it reality. You could not take the motive out of the atonement and leave it a religious truth. I count by far the most serious and difficult task of the preacher to give the sufficient motive to the truth he utters. Indeed, if he can really do that, he has gained a hearing for it, and given it its highest interpretation.

I sometimes question whether we have the right to preach until we have become so imbued with the motive of Scripture that we have the mind of the prophet under the utterance of his message from God. It was not so much the message which possessed him as it was the conception of the heart of God which the message disclosed: "Who is a God like unto thee, that pardoneth iniquity, and passeth by the transgression of the remnant of his heritage? He retaineth not his anger forever, for that he delighteth in mercy. He will turn again, he will have compassion on us; he will subdue our iniquities: and thou wilt cast all their sins into the depth of the sea." We preach God in his own blessed person, not his attributes, or his words, or his doings, chiefly. Our supreme message is God himself. As Paul says, over and over again, "We preach Christ." I think that it was Paul's apprehension of Christ which has given him such a place of influence in Christianity. More of the motive of Christianity is in his writings than we can find elsewhere. He never gets away, not in the furthest reaches of his logic, from the love of Christ. In this Paul is true to his date in the divine revelation. He comes into the divine thought as it becomes more urgent in the endeavor to save. We mistake if we think that the Bible advances from the sacrificial to the ethical. The advance, if the comparison is to be made at all under the idea of progress, is from the ethical to the sacrificial. That is, the motive of God comes out with a deeper promise and with a more irresistible power in the New Testament than in the Old. God comes near to man, surrenders more, not of righteousness, but of himself, to reach man, suffers more for man. The sermon on the mount holds all the ethics of the commandments; but from the sermon on the mount to the passion and death of Jesus, what an advance there is in the motive power of the gospel! Allow me to quote from what I have elsewhere written on this point: —

"The method of Jesus was sacrificial, — ethical certainly, but not to the exclusion or subordination of the sacrificial. And the proof of this lies in his treatment of the principle and idea of sacrifice. When we begin to study the method of Jesus we are startled to find that he reversed the whole course and current of sacrifice. The great volume of sacrifice had been pouring through innumerable channels from the heart of man into the heart of God. Christ met and overwhelmed the sacrifice of man with the sacrifice of God. It was the inflowing tide of the ocean staying and returning the waters from river and creek which were seeking its bosom. The act of Jesus was an act of sublime daring. We instinctively ask, Who is it who dares to make this reversal? Who is it that bids men cease their propitiatory rites? Who is it that puts out the fires on sacrificial altars and stanches the blood of sacrificial victims? It is He who carries out the change in his own person and offers himself the Lamb of God, which taketh away the sin of the world."

The failure of merely ethical religions is that they lack motive. We can see that fact when it is set forth on a large scale.

It is equally a fact when the ethical is the sole power in a man's preaching. He has not come into the permanent power of the Bible. He has not caught the secret of Christianity. He is not giving the truth its full chance with men through the proper and sufficient use of motive.

I must not fail to remind you, or to insist upon the fact, that there is need of a constant education on the part of both preacher and people in the use of motive. A motive may meet a man where it finds him, and be sufficient to work a great change in his life. It does not follow that it is the sufficient motive for his after years. It is difficult to arrange motives in order. We should place fear below love; but the soul which has been won by love may advance into the fear of sin, and in a very true sense into the fear of God. It is, however, certain that a change of life, which takes place through a fear of consequences, has not arrived at the dignity or honor or security which ought to come in through the advance in motive. The distinctively Christian motive is gratitude. " The life which I now live I live by faith of the Son of God, who loved me, and gave himself up for me." Gratitude is altogether unselfish, and it knows no limits in the measure of its obligations. There is nothing which a profoundly grateful Christian will not do. His gratitude carries with it the whole argument for consistency. What should not one be ready to give up, or to seek to accomplish, who has been reclaimed by Christ, and is thoroughly conscious of the fact?

Prudential motives are not excluded from the gospel. A man has the same right to escape from sin, and for the same reason, that he would escape from any evil or injury. Motives of self-respect are not excluded from the gospel. The gospel makes its appeal to men on the ground that they are worth too much to themselves, and to other men, and to God, to waste themselves in sinning. Neither are motives which centre in happiness. There is a joy inseparable from right doing. All these motives are in place, and may be timely. But the principle in the use of motives for one's self, or for others, should be that of advance. Life consists not only in doing better things, or doing the same right things in a better way, but also in doing them for a better reason. It is this alone which explains the change in some people when they become Christians. They keep on doing the very same things. They do not change their business. They do not change, of necessity, their methods. They have changed their motives, and in the light of that change all life has been purified, refined, and ennobled. It is this which explains the growth in so many Christians. They are acting from higher and higher reasons. The lower reasons have been supplanted. Their lives are growing in unity. They are reaching the Christian standard. I cannot make too much of the power of motive rightly applied, first to change men, and then to purify and increase their lives. And a great deal of the quality of this power depends upon the quality of the motive in the thought of the preacher. One preacher will secure large tangible results by the use of lower motives; another preacher will secure equally large and tangible results by the use of the higher motives.

Does any one question where the advantage lies?

These, then, are the responsibilities, as I conceive, of the preacher to the truth. He is commissioned to get a hearing for the truth. He has no right to be satisfied with a meagre response. God has given him the truth, the freedom of his personality, and means to be used according to his own invention. He is to see that the truth is rightly interpreted, that no type of mind is excluded by reason of its limitations, and that every hospitable mind is filled to the full. And he is allowed to share in the very motive of God himself in the utterance of truth. A part of his education is made to consist in the appreciation and use of the highest motives. And the reward of his ceaseless persuasion of men is to be found in the quality of the new life which he gives back to God as the result of his ministry.

VI

WHAT THE PREACHER OWES TO MEN

IF the responsibility of the preacher to the truth is sacred, no less sacred is his responsibility to men. I do not know which obligation is the more difficult to satisfy. Probably it varies with the preacher himself. With one man, the ardor for truth surpasses the passion for men. With another, the love of men exceeds in urgency, at least, the love of truth. I should say, however, that the distinguishing characteristic of the preacher was his feeling toward men. Others may share to the full his feeling toward the truth, scholars, inquirers, believers, but few are able to come into like sensitive relation to the human soul.

What does the preacher owe to men? How shall we take the measure of his obligation?

Let me begin with what is fundamental. If I cannot ground the obligation of the preacher to men in something deeper and firmer than sentiment, my words can have little meaning.

The first thing, then, which the preacher owes to men is the clear understanding and unconditional acceptance of Christ's view of humanity. Christ's estimate of men, his way of looking at men, his whole conception of humanity, must become a part of the preacher's thinking, the very habit of his mind. What was Christ's estimate of humanity? What was the contribution which Christ made to man's thought of himself, to the thought which the race might have of itself? Jesus Christ gave to the human race that new conception of itself which, as fast as it has been apprehended, man by man, has been changing the order of the world. It was a religious conception, but it had other than religious uses. It was good for all the possible needs of humanity. It was the simple but then rare conception, every man a child of God. That truth gave every man a standing in the world. It was fundamental. It was communicable. It was part of the glad tidings. And as it went abroad under the sanction of religion, it was commissioned to do any work for man to which he was entitled as a child of God. The question is often asked, Why did not Christ say something directly about slavery, about political tyranny, about any of the specific wrongs of his age? The sufficient answer is that he said the one word which could avail for his own age, and which could not be superseded in time.

This word of Christ is now almost lost in the commonplace, but at its time it brought in the one value which had always been wanting. Man had never had any value to himself as man. Man had had standing in the world, but not as man. History had been the record of heroes only, not even of peoples. Ordinary men were of no account. When, therefore, Christ put this new valuation upon man, partly through what he was in himself, partly through what he did and suffered, and partly through the idea which he sent abroad into all the world, it was inevitable that history must be written in a new language.

I would that I could take this truth of Jesus out of the commonplace of our religious thinking and make it real to you in its original meaning. Let me recall a paragraph from a book which you have been reading of late, which brings out the apparent impossibility of the new idea as it came into the world. I quote from the letter of the Roman philosopher and man of the world, Petronius, to his young friend Vinicius, who had urged upon him the Christian faith, to which he had become a convert: —

"No, Vinicius, thy religion is not for me. Am I to love the Bithynians who carry my litter, the Egyptians who heat my bath? I swear by the white knees of the Graces that if I wished to love them I could not. In Rome there are a hundred thousand persons at least who have either crooked shoulders or big knees, or thin thighs, or staring eyes, or heads that are too large. Dost thou command me to love them, too? Where am I to find the love, since it is not in my heart? And if thy God desires me to love such persons, why in his all might did he not give them the form of Niobe's children, for example, which thou hast seen on the Palatine? Who loves beauty is for that very reason unable to love deformity."

Whatever exaggerations the book from which I have quoted may hold, this protest is no exaggeration of the pagan feeling toward man as man. The virtues which Christianity enjoined — love the forgiveness of enemies, and the like — seemed impossible virtues. And all for the reason that man as man had no standing in the world. Even the greatest and best men had taken little pride in their humanity. Sometimes it seems as if it were still so. It is so much more to be a philosopher, an orator, a ruler, a maker of money, or manager of affairs, any one of these things, than to be simply great in one's humanity! You can see, then, the difficulty which Christ must have had in introducing this principle, and of making it actually an accepted truth, first to make the best men believe it of themselves and act upon it, changing their ideals and also their ambitions and desires, and then to make them believe it of others, this Pharisee of this publican, this Greek of this barbarian, this master of this slave; and then to make these other men believe it of themselves, these men who could not idealize themselves, who had no sense of the meaning and worth of the human, to make them believe that they, too, were sons of God, and had a standing in God's world.

And the difficulty is still immense. It is for this reason that I am saying so much about it. It is so hard to get at the idea of Christ in its perfect simplicity, and hold it in its right proportions. We are apt to pass to one extreme or the other in our thought of men. The pagan's estimate was based on his natural or trained likes and dislikes. He loved the beautiful, he honored the heroic. For the opposites he had only contempt or hate. The Christian is apt to go to the other extreme, to estimate his Christianity altogether by its power to overcome his dislikes or hates. For the exercise of love he relies upon the incitement of pity. He waits the appeal which comes to him from want or misery or sin. We have come to count it a virtue to love men according to the incidents in their character or conditions. It was this principle which led Cardinal Manning to pass his generous encomium upon the Salvation Army as the only considerable body of Christians who had ever shown a passion for sinners just because they were sinners. Now Christ's position is very much broader and more fundamental than either of these. The estimate which he enjoins is not simply respect for high attainment, nor pity for low condition. It unites the recognition and acknowledgment and support of the fact, let it go where it will, — every man a child of God.

What! must I love the man who does not need me, who has no outward wants which are unsatisfied, this rich man, perchance, who is entirely independent of me, and with whom I have no tastes in common? Certainly; otherwise why am I any broader than the Roman who could not love the Bithynians who carried his litter, or the Egyptians who heated his bath?

Do you not see the difficulty of accepting Christ's estimate, the difficulty of even understanding it? And yet there it is, the very first thing which meets us in Christianity, just as plain as the view which he gave us of God. I cannot lay too much stress upon this obligation to think of and look upon every man as a child of God. I speak of it as expressed in the estimate or conception we have of men, rather than in a doctrine about men. We are apt to retire our doctrines. They represent the truth we have on deposit. They fulfill a very needful and substantial office in this respect. But we need also thoughts, views, estimates, which are never apart from us, which we always take with us on the street, and into the house, the office, and the shop.

We must allow a large liberty in the application of so great and difficult a principle. It is not possible for one man to think of his fellowman precisely as another man may think of him. Temperaments vary. We are allowed to reach the same ends by different methods. One of the most human preachers of our time, a man whose name was almost a synonym for the human, once said to a friend, "I love man and hate men." That was not so bad a saying as it appears to be on its face. His love worked from the ideal into the real, from man down into men, overcoming on its way his natural dislikes. This is the opposite in method of the love which shows itself first in interest in cases. Objects of pity or commiseration come before one. One begins to be interested in them. Interest spreads from the individual to the class. Finally it comes out into a great generalization.

I recall a fine example of the latter and more common method in the person of a well-known philanthropist of New York, who for more than half a century followed the lead of individual want and suffering into the class which it might represent. The personal relief of the poor brought to light the child of poverty, the child of poverty led the way to his crippled brother, the diseased child pointed to the suffering mother. When I knew my honored friend, he had passed his threescore and ten years. An incident associated with his greatest personal bereavement revealed to me the whole spirit of his life. As I called upon him in his sorrow, he took me after a little into the presence of his dead, and there talked as only the voice of love and age could speak. Suddenly he stopped, put his hand in his pocket and took out a check. "There," he said, "is a check for twenty-five thousand from Mrs. Stewart for my woman's hospital." Then, resuming the conversation as if there had been no interruption, there really had been none, he covered the face of his dead, and withdrew to take up again in its time his now solitary but still joyous course.

The preacher's obligation to men, upon which I have thus far insisted, shows itself chiefly in the breadth of its application. Let me now urge the necessity for a certain intensity in the exercise of it. The obligation cannot be satisfied with the love for men which does not have in it the element of devotion or passion. In this regard it simply demands what is the real characteristic of love in any circumstance. You have the suggestion of my meaning in a line from one of the recent poems of Stephen Phillips. It is the reply of the earth maiden as she rejects the suit of Apollo on the ground that his love for her would surely wane, and this would be the sign of it: —

"Thou wouldst grow kind,
Most bitter to a woman who was loved."

"Kindness" is a good word, a word of gentle quality, but the very thoughtfulness which it implies, the premeditation which it assumes, may defeat the large end of love. Kindness is not that irresistible, conquering power that love is. It may awaken gratitude and create a permanent sense of obligation, but it does not really overcome and capture the soul.

The preacher will certainly come short of fulfilling his obligation to men if his love for them does not rise to the strength of a spiritual passion for them. It must be utterly devoid of sentimentalism. That is too weak a thing to speak about. It must be a strong, manly passion, but it must have the ardor of the soul in it. And this alike in public and private, when the preacher is dealing with men under conditions which invite it. Passion is something which has its times and seasons. It is not for all times, nor for all subjects in the pulpit, nor for all the circumstances which invite the preacher's attention. There must be a proportion in the expression of love. Usually the man who has it in any real depth of feeling will give the fit expression to it. It will come forth spontaneously, and according to the real demand for it. There is nothing so impressive as the irrepressible outburst of feeling on the part of a man whose feelings are usually under strong restraint.

The obligation of the preacher to men, let me say further, has one of its most timely expressions in sympathy. That is the exact quality which is called for in our time more than any other. It meets the general situation as nothing else can. It gives the preacher access where otherwise access will certainly be denied him. The preacher, as we have seen, if he has caught the secret of his Master, has learned to pay his respects to humanity in whomsoever it may be represented, and at any cost. Respect is the prince of influence. It is the respecting element in Christianity, more than the pitying element, which is the peculiar sign of its power. Sympathy measures the respect we feel for those who are in circumstances and conditions below us. It is a very different quality from pity, or from charity in any of its common forms. It is the recognition of the human element which survives poverty and even degradation; it is the acknowledgment of the underlying equality between man and man beneath all varying conditions; it is the appreciation of the endeavor and ambition to rise to higher levels; it is above all the willingness to make room for men as they rise, and to welcome them to the places which they have earned. Pity ceases when the object of commiseration has been lifted a little out of the low estate. Charity, which gives alms, follows a little way above in the ascending scale. Sympathy attends the man all the way up till he has reached the level of his manhood.

Now it is perfectly evident that the moral solvent of the present social situation is not pity, it is not charity in any of its common manifestations, it is sympathy. Analyze the situation, study society where the struggle is going on, and you will discover two clearly defined movements, the upward and the downward; one class ascending, the other descending the social scale, and yet not far apart. On the one hand the worn-out, the demoralized, the degraded, falling steadily to the bottom; on the other hand a certain vital element gradually emerging from the common mass, freeing itself from base surroundings, organizing for self-protection and self-advancement, and finally able to stand with comparative security and lend a helping hand to those in the crude mass about it. Compare now the attitude of the church toward the upward and the downward movements, and you see at once that it shows far more charity for the falling, than sympathy with the rising class. On occasion like that of the strike of the East London dockers, or the coal strike in England for the living wage, sympathy is shown as well as charity. But, as a rule, sympathy in distinction from charity is absent; and it is the absence of this precious quality which makes the breach between what is known collectively as labor and the church. The average workingman gives his money, his time, and his loyalty to his association or brotherhood, and looks on with indifference or amusement while the religious world discusses the reasons why men like himself do not fill the churches. If I were discussing the attitudes of labor organizations I might have something to say of their spirit, but the divine function of the church is sympathy, the highest possible expression of its enthusiasm for humanity. And judging the church of to-day by this test I cannot claim for it that it satisfies in any reasonable degree the requirement of its Founder. The average man within the church does not understand the average man without, who may be estranged from the church, nor does he take pains to understand him. He may know the man on his own social level without, but not the man estranged, and who has his complaint.

The preacher interprets the situation largely through his sympathy. And in the proper expression of it he does the most which in him lies to make Christianity real to men who have misunderstood its attitude. And in the use of sympathy the preacher puts Christianity in right relation to the social and political order of which we are a part. The general social and political order bears the name of democracy.

Democracy means, if it means anything in a Christian way, the sympathy of one man with another. The kind of equality which it stands for covers every lower form or expression of Christianity.

One of the most delicate obligations which the preacher comes under to men is not only to believe in them himself, but also to restore the faith which they may have lost in themselves. A preacher learns with time not to take men at their own estimates, and especially not to take too seriously the deprecatory words of some men about themselves. A great many men are talking skepticism who are not skeptical. Let the preacher waste no words on such. But there are those with whom loss of faith in themselves is real, and to outward appearance justifiable. They have fallen in self-respect, and their own opinion has been accepted and confirmed by their fellows. The saddest word in literature is the word attributed to Lord Byron: "Men took me to be what I said I was, and I came to be what they thought I was." Society may have made haste to accept a foolish name or reputation which a man may have given himself, and obliged him therefore to justify it. A preacher has no right to take any man's word about himself or the word of society about him as final. Jesus Christ alone speaks the final word. Until that has been spoken, let the preacher believe and act in his name.

The majority of cases may be against one's faith in men. Grant that. There is still the minority. Who knows in advance how the man, who is most faithless in himself, and most hopeless to others, is to be classified? This may be optimism. It is also Christianity.

The wide obligation, however, of the preacher to the individual man, whoever he may be, who comes under his influence, is that of interest in the welfare of his soul. As there can be no motive so great, so there can be no equal and corresponding obligation like that which comes out of the realized value of the human soul. It is really the unknown factor in human nature, which is so much more than the known. It is the great item in the mystery of life. What makes the mystery to us of the future state? Chiefly the fact that for ages the tide of human life has been flowing into it. It is a world peopled with souls which once had a home on this green earth. The future represents the value of the soul measured by duration. There are other measures, but above all the measure of equality, the measure of influence, the measure of use. No one can settle the question whether one soul is of more meaning to himself or to others. We cannot go beyond the word of Paul, " No man liveth unto himself, and no man dieth unto himself." When therefore the preacher thinks of the worth of any soul before him, it cannot be in its separateness. It is a unit, but a unit in countless and vital combinations.

I do not reach too far into the pastoral relations when I urge this interest in every one's soul, because in this regard the pastor and preacher are one. One of the most serious questions which a preacher can ask himself is this: What am I doing when I am not preaching? Where are my thoughts, my plans, my imperative desires and longings? Towards what ends am I pushing with the constant energies of my nature?

Preaching is not an end, but it is very easy to make it an end. Most preachers do make it a chief end, in that they make it the climax of their energy and thought and spiritual purpose. The strong tides of their spiritual being do not underrun their preaching, flowing out with it into the great life toward which it points. Dr. Pentecost has told this of himself. He was preaching at one time in the presence of Dr. Bonar, enjoying, as a man will, the luxury of proclaiming the gospel. Dr. Bonar came to him at the close, touched him on the shoulder, and said, "You love to preach, don't you?" "Yes, I do." "Do you love men to whom you preach?" That was a much deeper question, and it is worth every man's asking, when he finds himself more in love with the truth, or with the proclamation of it, than with men to whom, and for whom, the truth has been revealed.

There is a love of men which the sermon cannot satisfy. And the right to preach to men carries with it other rights in their behalf. Preaching is simply the acknowledged sign, the warrant of what Bushnell calls "the property rights we have in souls."

The man, therefore, as he follows after the preacher is not a spiritual impertinence. He may of course make himself such, but not if he acts wisely and tenderly, and above all things manfully. It is the habit of some preachers to follow the sermon with the personal letter, others with timely conversation, others with the opportunity of the after meeting. In some cases these personal methods may not be necessary. Preaching may be so quickening as to create of itself an office practice for the preacher. Those who have listened to his words may be so awakened and stimulated that they will come to him and ask him for further help in the life of the soul.

When a preacher has made a man aware of his soul, then comes the work of helping him to save it. And when that is well begun then the long task of showing him how to use his soul. This is the continuous work of the preacher; this the work of edification, the building up of character, through the right and noble use of the powers of the whole nature. Preaching to this end, as you can well see, must be thoroughly constructive and stimulating.

It must point out ways of helpfulness, and set the feet of men in them. It must show the opportunities which attend every advance in this life, every gain in knowledge, all increase in riches, all growths in reputation or influence. It must hold secure to the great consistencies, honesty, justice, charity of mind as well as of heart, nobility of thought and of ambition, humility, and, if need be, self-sacrifice.

I had hoped that I might be able to say something about the relation of the preacher to men in combination, that is, to society, without exceeding the proper length of this lecture, or breaking its unity. But I find that I must reserve what I would otherwise say now to my next lecture on the pulpit and the church.

Before I close I wish to go back to gather up a phrase which I quoted from Dr. Bushnell, namely, the property rights which we have in souls. It would not be altogether fair to insist, as I have done, upon the obligations under which we stand to men, so strong and severe, so hard to fulfill, so hard even to understand, without showing in a word how the fulfillment of them goes into the making of the preacher. The preacher cannot hope to make any lasting contribution to the truth. Most sermons are a waste, viewed as literature. Some go out into their generation and gain a wide constituency. Here and there a sermon lives in tradition. It did something that men never cease to admire and wonder at, though they may be no longer impressed by it. Occasionally a sermon goes over. Some preachers cover two generations, their own and the next.

But as the preacher tries to reckon the permanent in his work, as he stops from time to time, as he surely will, to ask himself what does it all mean to him, his only sure and satisfactory answer will come from men. His property rights are there. There are his spiritual earnings. The return into his life is out of the life of men, first, in what they are, changed in the direction of their purposes, or changed in the level of their aspirations; then in what they have done, the better deed in place of the low or base, or in place of no deed at all — the helpful, saving word in place of the unspoken, unthought word of brotherly kindness and charity. Something of all this finds its way back into the preacher's consciousness, and helps him to preach. And if men do not tell him, let him not be faithless and unbelieving. A preacher is entitled to the full advantage of the known and unknown results of his ministry. The unknown, I say; for one may be sure that if there be known results there will be unknown results, with the probability, yes, the certainty, that the unknown will exceed the known. That goes with the nature of the service. And sometimes a glimpse into the unknown, a message from the unexpected, though it be of another's work, tells him what to believe of himself and of his own work.

Canon Twells, in one of his colloquies on Preaching, introduces his readers to a conversation between a rector and a vicar on results in preaching. The conversation opens with a bit of raillery, but as it proceeds it grows more serious. At one point the rector falls into a desponding mood, like Bunyan's Christian, and the vicar plays the part of Bunyan's Hopeful. The colloquy closes with this incident, told by the vicar : —

"A friend of mine, a layman, was once in the company of a very eminent preacher, then in the decline of life. My friend happened to remark what a comfort it must be to think of all the good he had done by his gift of eloquence. The eyes of the old man filled with tears. 'You little know! You little know! If I ever turned one heart from the ways of disobedience to the wisdom of the just, God has withheld the assurance from me. I have been admired and flattered and run after; but how gladly I would forget all that, to be told of one single soul I have been instrumental in saving!' The eminent preacher entered into his rest. There was a great funeral. Many passed around the grave who had oftentimes hung entranced upon his lips. My friend was there, and by his side was a stranger, who was so deeply moved that when all was over my friend said to him, 'You knew him, I suppose?' 'Knew him,' was the reply, 'no; I never spoke to him, but I owe to him my soul.'"

VII

THE PULPIT AND THE CHURCH

IF the question were asked under some forms of Christianity, what is the determining factor in the making or the unmaking of the preacher? the answer would be, the church. In saying this, I do not refer, of course, to those forms of Christianity which practically obliterate preaching. Ritualism has no logical place for preaching, because in its conception of the church it makes no sufficient allowance for the personality of the preacher. The Church of Rome, it is to be said, whether logically or illogically, has always honored preaching. It has always kept great preachers at command, and has made special provision for their training.

But although I am not prepared to accept some theories of the church which are held under Protestant Christianity, where preaching still remains a power, I am desirous of emphasizing most clearly the relation of the preacher, as such, to the church. And if I do not speak of his obligation to the church in the same way in which I have spoken of his obligation to the truth and to men, it is because I conceive of his relation to it in another aspect. I want to show you how much the church means to the preacher, how it ministers to him, supports and strengthens him, how in its local organizations it offers itself to him to be used as a great agency or instrument for the advancement of righteousness, and how it becomes the reservoir into which he may pour his life, the institution into which he may build himself and his work.

It is the church, we are to remind ourselves at the outset, which gives to the preacher validity to his message. Formally this is effected through the preacher's ordination. That act authorizes him to stand before men in the name of the church, and to declare the truth under its sanctions. The church guarantees the character of the preacher, his fitness to speak, and in general the subject matter of his preaching, no mean advantage to any man at any time, but of incalculable value at the beginning of one's profession. No man starts upon his professional course with such a presumption in his favor as the preacher. The church creates that presumption. Ordination is far more to the minister than the sanction of one's profession which admits to the bar or to the practice of medicine. It carries with it an assurance, coöperation, and protection, for which there is no parallel.

I will take a moment's time to bring out the moral sympathy and support which underlie the ecclesiastical form. Let me contrast in this regard the prophet with the preacher. The prophet was an anointed man. There was a prophetic succession. But the prophet was a lonely man. He dwelt apart. He did not frequent the places where men came together, where life thickened and grew dense. He was a man of occasions. The infrequency of his appearances, his remoteness from the common ways, gave the power of mystery to his words. And the truth which he uttered was chiefly for occasions. It was not the every-day subject of the pulpit. It was not necessarily the unknown truth which he proclaimed, but it was the unapplied truth, the neglected truth. The prophet was strongest when he was armed with the antagonism of truth. His chief reliance was the awakened conscience. Recall the commission of Jeremiah: "Thou therefore gird up thy loins, and arise, and speak unto them all that I command thee: be not dismayed at their faces, lest I confound thee before them. For, behold, I have made thee this day a defensed city, and an iron pillar, and brazen walls against the whole land, against the kings of Judah, against the princes thereof, against the priests thereof, and against the people of the land. And they shall fight against thee; but they shall not prevail against thee; for I am with thee, saith the Lord, to deliver thee."

Preaching has in it the prophetic element. The preacher is charged to declare the whole counsel of God, and that, still, whether men will hear or will forbear to hear. There are times when denunciation must be strong and persistent, when a preacher must lift up his voice before a community and cry aloud and spare not. But that is the unusual work of the pulpit. Ordinarily the preacher speaks with the consenting voice of the church. The common truth which he utters is a part of the common experience. Preaching at its best is quite apt to be an interpretation of the Christian consciousness at its best. As the preacher rises in the utterance of his faith, men about him are saying, "Yes, that is what we have felt, but have never been able to tell. Go on, speak for us, that is our faith." Preaching on its interpretative and representative side is a recognized fact. The pulpit and the church cannot be separated in the minds of men. The validity of the preacher's message is more than that which comes from any ecclesiastical guarantee; it has in it the consenting, supporting, persuading life of the church.

Intimately connected with this direct power which the church confers upon the preacher is the aid which it affords him through various forms of religious impressions. Of course this is more apparent in the liturgical than in the non-liturgical churches, but the church always and everywhere creates an atmosphere which is unmistakable. Reduce the church in all its appointments to the minimum, let it be the old New England meeting-house, with a service as plain and bare as the walls of the house, still the impression is there. Do you not remember the fine touch in "Norwood," as Mr. Beecher describes the close of a service in the village church? The horse jockey of the village and the doctor have driven up, and are waiting for the congregation to come out. The jockey is talking glibly to the doctor about the neighbors' teams which are standing in the horse shed. Soon the last hymn is heard. "'There, doctor, there's the last hymn!' It rose upon the air, softened by distance and the inclosure of the building, rose and fell in regular movement. Even Hiram's tongue ceased. The vireo, in the top of the elm, hushed its shrill snatches. Again the hymn rose, and this time fuller and louder, as if the whole congregation had caught the spirit. Men's and women's voices, and little children's, were in it. Hiram said, without any of his usual pertness: 'Doctor, there's somethin' in folks' singin' when you are outside the church that makes you feel as though you ought to be inside.'"

The art of religious impression as it has been developed by the church invites the study of the preacher. I assume that you approach the subject without prejudice. Puritanism no longer exists as a protest against form in worship. The Puritan of to-day is not at this point the purifier. The last determined opposition to the enrichment of worship of which I had personal knowledge was in the case of a clergyman of the old school, who, after the anthem had been introduced into the service of his church against his will, used to rise immediately at the close, and say, "We will *now* begin the worship of God by the use of such a hymn."

The difficulty to-day in the non-liturgical churches lies in the cheap imitation, or in the inartistic substitute. Nothing is so appalling to a reverent mind as the introduction of the programme into so many churches. Instead of an order of service we have a musical exhibition, which takes the fortune of the taste of the musical committee of the society. It was a Sunday evening performance of this sort which brought out the famous bit of caricature from Dr. Burton, closing with the "final bellowings of the organ, after which darkness, silence, and the restored presence of God."

Where shall we look for our protection against these tendencies? Partly to the people themselves whose tastes are being refined, and who are becoming more able to discriminate between the true and the false in art, but chiefly to the ministry, as it is being trained to the appreciation, if not to the full knowledge, of the art of spiritual impression. I put the preacher especially on his guard against the usurpation by the sermon of the prerogatives of worship. Let him beware of thinking of anything which precedes the sermon as a part of the "preliminary service." With all the stress which I have laid upon preaching, I do not exalt it above the other great office of worship. Above all, let the preacher remember, that in the simplicity of our order of faith he is the priest as well as the preacher. It is as needful for him to enter the pulpit in the spirit of devotion as in the spirit of convincement or persuasion. The sermon ought not to dominate his mind so that he cannot pray without reading his sermon into his prayer. Of course the danger is greater from the extempore than from the written sermon. Yet in either case the mind may be so possessed by a given subject that it is inhospitable to the thousand desires and longings which are to find expression in prayer, if the minister is to interpret the heart of the congregation.

Pardon a personal reference. Early in my ministry, as I was endeavoring to train myself toward extempore speech, I found that the most serious drawback was the preoccupation of mind with the thought of the sermon during the period of worship. The difficulty became so great that I determined to free my mind of the sermon for that time at any cost, and as I had no verbal memory, I resolved to write into the sermon, to the amount of five or six minutes, and read what I had written, passing then into the method of extempore speech. The precaution thus taken became a habit, — a most vicious habit as far as the method of preaching was concerned, — but a concession on the part of the sermon to worship, which I accounted none too great a price for me to pay. The methods of two personal friends of which I chance to have knowledge are better. One of them is in the habit of entering the pulpit an hour before the service, and of going over the congregation in mind, family by family, endeavoring to call up their spiritual necessities with so great definiteness and vividness that his prayer may be their prayer. The other has made a profound study of the liturgies of the churches, not for the form but for the spirit of worship. He does not memorize, he does not imitate, but he does seek to enter into the mind of the church as in its collective thought, or in the thought of its most devout souls, it has turned toward God.

I advise the careful study of the devotional habit of the church. The preacher who is unsupported by any formal expression of the life of the church in worship ought to be the more careful that he has the true supports within himself. And he ought to be able to gain every advantage which is open to him in the genuine and unaffected use of the art of spiritual expression. Let no man think that he can preach so well that it matters little how he prays, or how the congregation worships. It matters much how the best preachers pray and how the congregations which listen to them worship. I recall a remark of Professor Ladd after he came out from listening to Phillips Brooks. "The congregation," he said, "was alive." The attitude and mood of the congregation impressed him equally with the spiritual earnestness of the preacher. I have come away under the same impression on the two or three occasions when I have attended St. George's Church in New York.

I cannot overestimate the value to the preacher, as the preacher, of the devotional spirit of the congregation. It is an inspiration. Psalm and hymn, anthem and chant, Scripture and creed and prayer, whatever touches the heart of the congregation and makes it one before God, will minister to him in all his spiritual nature, if he will allow himself to become responsive to it. The church, through its aroused emotion, has opened the way into the individual heart for the entrance of his message.

Not only does the church give validity to the message of the preacher, not only does it support him through the power of religious impression, it gives to his work the advantage of definite results. So far as the pulpit represents the oratorical temperament, there is constant danger that its force will be spent in the excitement of feeling. A great many preachers leave their hearers aroused, but undirected and unutilized. They stir to duty, but they point out no duties to be accomplished, nor do they show how duty may be done. Perhaps this is the most common weakness in what is otherwise very effective preaching. The church offers the best possible corrective for this weakness. It makes it possible for the preacher to locate duty. It presents the opportunity in various ways for one who has been quickened to right doing to begin at once to put it into practice. It is the office of the church to take the individual life from the moment when it begins to reach out after Christ, and train it to discipleship; to give it congenial associations; to provide it with appropriate incentives and with appropriate opportunity for growth; to open to it paths of service. Where else and how else can the soul make so natural and complete a commitment of itself to Christ? The confession of Christ is the fit response to the conclusion of a large part of the sermons of the preacher even when they do not end in the direct appeal. The covenant of the church shows the true and proper relation into which one is to come with others who are like-minded and of the same purpose. And when once the first step has been taken in the acknowledgment of Christ and in association with Christians, then the church stands for direction, helpfulness, responsibility, and enlargement through the fulfillment of duty.

What an utterly wasteful and extravagant force the pulpit would be but for the church which follows after the preacher and gathers up and utilizes his power.

Compare the work of the evangelist in this regard with that of the pastor. The power of impression on the part of the evangelist is greater for the immediate time than that of the pastor. But if his work is detached it is in large degree dissipated. I do not overestimate statistics, but, judged by any of the large tests which centre in permanent results, the evangelist has little to show when his work is compared with that of the pastor, unless it is associated with that of the pastor. The church stands for economy in the use of means. It prevents waste. It makes preaching fruitful. And the effect of this function of the church upon the preacher is encouraging in the highest degree. No one can be indifferent to results. The secret grief at the heart of many a minister is the apparent absence of any adequate result of his preaching. While he is in the act of presenting truth, when mind and heart are aglow, he enters into the joy of his calling. But as the years of his ministry go by without the return to him in changed lives, in an enlarged church, in results which are definite and tangible, his heart begins to fail and grow weary. I have known preachers to be saved to themselves and to their churches by the efforts of some quiet, patient workers in the church who have known how to gather the fruitage of the pulpit. They have given the preacher the one advantage, without which his ministry must have steadily declined into a failure. With it he has risen to his task in the courage of spiritual success.

And now add to these advantages the sense of permanency which the church helps to give, and you see how large is its ministry to the preacher. A great many things tend to give the preacher the sense of change, uncertainty, and even of insecurity in his work. Men come and go. Sometimes the fortune of a particular church seems to be bound up in a given generation. Churches lose their position or character. The preacher himself is seldom a permanent force in any one community. All the outward conditions are away from the permanent. Yet the real significance of his work is permanence. How shall he realize this fact? He may live as the patriarchs lived. Abraham dwelt in tents with Isaac and Jacob, but he looked for a city which hath foundations. The preacher has the outlook of faith open to him. That gives the last satisfaction. It is the realization of eternity underneath time, the realization, as Carlyle says, that " time in every meanest moment of it rests upon eternity." But this is the common privilege of faith. The preacher has no more claim to it than any other believer. What is his hold upon the permanent, as we count permanence on earth? The church is an institution. The ministry is a succession. The preacher has his fellowship without limit of time. How near the great souls of the church of long ago are to us. How easy it is for us to establish the intimacy of personal friendship with them. How hospitable they are, how catholic, how sincere. They live and their work lives. Measured by earthly standards the church lasts.

> " Oh, where are kings and empires now,
> Of old that went and came?
> But, Lord, thy church is praying yet,
> A thousand years the same."

I think that we fail to inhabit the church at large as we ought. Our particular communion is small, it is a part, a small part, but a part implies the whole, a small part as much as a great part. In my Father's house, said Christ, are many mansions. Why should we not take the freedom of them here? And especially in respect to time. What age of the church is closed against us? Where should we be unwelcome now, whatever might have been our fortune then? Who shall forbid to any one of us his sense of permanency in the church, according to the place he may make for himself in the unfailing succession?

It would be easy to enter into the long enumeration of the advantages of the church to the preacher, if he will but recognize them. But all that I have wished to do is to turn your thoughts that way. I have wanted to help you to see that the church is carrying on a wide and generous ministry in your behalf. Some of its ministries I have suggested. Nothing more than the suggestion of them is necessary, if it shall succeed in making you appreciative of what the church is capable of doing and will do for the ministry, if its offices are recognized and accepted.

What now shall we say is the relation of the pulpit to the church? What are the preacher's obligations? How shall he use his advantage honestly, generously, and to his own upbuilding? My first answer is that the preacher should work from within the church. Let him not take an outside position, nor one as near the edge as possible, but let him establish himself within, firmly and securely, and then work from within out.

This statement is so general that it raises questions of its own. How far is the position of the preacher representative and how far is it personal? Is he bound to utter the formulæ of the church, or does he have the freedom of Christianity? And if he insists upon his freedom does he forfeit his place in the church? I suppose that by common consent the preacher is the freest man in the service of the church. He is given, for necessary and evident reasons, the largest use of his personality. The church is always ready to allow the exercise of liberty, when it seems to be an indispensable part of the preacher's apprehension of the gospel. Probably no one is judged so fairly, by the whole scope and aim of his work, as the preacher. But when the preacher rests his contention for liberty upon some one point, a point now of doctrine rather than of personal enlargement, then he makes the contention for others as well as for himself. At least, if the point is of sufficient importance to really contend for in the name of freedom, it ought to be sufficient to contend for in the interest of truth. If again the truth which the church holds seems to him to need a large interpretation, I think that he ought to try to make room for it in the church. The liberty of being allowed to stretch one's self a little further, of being a little freer than others, is, after all, a small notion of liberty. Real liberty consists in making the church roomy enough for all men who want to hold the interpretation of the truth in question. That is something worth contending for. To give a broad truth standing, that makes all men free. To make one man free, and leave the truth in bondage, that leaves other men bound.

I believe, therefore, that if a preacher wants a liberty beyond that which is usually conceded to the use of one's personality, he ought first to ask whether other men ought to have it, whether it inheres in the truth itself, and if so, then to try to make room for it in the church. I have little respect for mere assertion and boisterous independence. I have great respect for the serious and responsible endeavor for freedom. And there is no loyalty to the church, of which I am aware, which compels a man who feels the need, for himself, and for others, and for the truth, of more room and a larger freedom to go outside to get it. It is time enough to go out when it is proven that there is not sufficient room within.

But suppose the question includes the conduct of a given church rather than the faith of the church of which it is a part. Suppose a church stands before a community charged with inconsistency. Its spiritual life is too low to impress the community, or its moral life is such as to leave it without influence. I do not refer now to cases of personal discipline, which must always be judged by themselves. I refer altogether to the moral or spiritual condition of a church which makes it powerless for good. It is worldly, it is frivolous, it is niggardly, it is out of favor with the community, and rightly so. What shall the preacher do? Shall he work on the outside the church, as far as possible independent of it, or shall he still work from it, taking his position within? Certainly the latter. Let him enter all the more closely into its life. Let him lavish upon it all the wealth of his affection. Let him not play the Pharisee before the people at large, and draw attention to his own superior breadth, or charity, or earnestness. Let him give himself to the task of making the church broader, more charitable, more earnest, more human. Let him bring the best life of the church to the front; let him encourage, stimulate, and inspire. That must be a dead church which will not revive under such treatment. When it has been revived, the preacher holds its power in the hollow of his hand. The true philosophy of the relation of the pulpit to the church is that of power from within. The preacher who has not first made his place strong and secure, who has not made himself a vital force within, has not established the relation of the pulpit to the church.

Next to the obligation of the preacher to work from the church, that is, from within, I put the obligation to work through the church. A great many churches are willing to let the preacher work for them. They offer him, that is, not only as their representative, but as their substitute. That is not to be allowed. If the preacher will avail himself of the instinct of helpfulness, he can readily get people enough to work with him. They will not always work under him if the authority is too manifest, but they will work with him. What matters it, so that they work, and he works through them? It is too much to expect that all preachers will be good organizers. Organization is of advantage, but there may be too much of it. Machinery in a church is not a certain sign of strength. Some churches are more cumbered by it than a knight in mediæval armor. The secret of pastoral success on the executive side is the ability to secure coöperation. This implies first a policy. A church must know what it stands for, what it is expected to do. The policy must be made clear, and definite, and commanding. It must be a sufficient policy. A church must not be asked to do less than it is capable of doing. Nothing is so belittling as a weak, or small, or uninspiring policy. Ask for large things and expect them. And keep on asking and expecting, till you get them. Educate your people out of littleness, as you would out of meanness.

A good policy will gain the support of good people. That is pretty sure to follow. Men and women will lend themselves to the duty which is attractive because it is satisfying. They will try to do it. Trust them in their endeavors. Distrust on your part is worse than blunders on their part. Remember that you had to learn to preach. It was not second nature. For two or three years it may have been an open problem whether the man would conquer the sermon, or the sermon would kill the man. It is not always easy for a man who is greatly gifted in public speech to speak in a social meeting or to pray. It may be still harder for him to say the personal word to his neighbor. It is not easy for some men to give, not so easy for those who have money as for those who haven't it. Be patient. It may not be easy for some men to stand as moral reformers. Not all men are brave. Be patient still. Courage, like everything else, grows by success. It is easier to stand, when one has once seen that it has done some good to stand for the right.

And not only have a sufficient policy, and show a sufficient trust in men, but take to yourselves the joy of companionship in service. Respect those who labor with you. Encourage them by your personal as well as by your official regard. Respect them according to their gifts. And rejoice in any discovery of Christian talent, as you would rejoice in personal wealth. Some persons may become representative of the church in larger ways of service than in those which the local church has to offer. Do not be jealous of their outside activity or influence. Let them understand that they are doing the work of the church in the best possible way. The only way in which the church can deal with many questions, and many interests, is through its representative men. You cannot make a church support one party, or one policy, in a community. There are limits to concerted action, chief of which is the individual liberty of opinion and of conscience. But you can count as a continual power in the church any noble-minded man who rises to the demands of public duty.

And one more obligation of the pulpit to the church is that the preacher shall work to it. From it, in acknowledgment of its position; through it, in acknowledgment of its available power; to it, in acknowledgment of its right to its own increase. The church is entitled to the earnings of the ministry. And the larger the earnings the more the church is entitled to them. A small increase might come about from other incentives. A large and steady increase can come only from and through the church. And yet one obligation which the preacher owes the church is to see to it that the church does not narrow its doors. The church is for the world, not the world for the church. It is hard to maintain this principle under all conditions. Churches, like corporations, like individuals, grow selfish. Success is apt to develop satisfaction. Struggle is apt to develop narrowness. The preacher out of love to the church must see to it that it is set wide toward humanity. This does not mean that it has no tests of membership, no standards of character, no confession of faith. Open the church that way, and you make it no object for men to enter. You must make the motive to enter the church as deep as you make the entrance broad.

There is one difficulty in our American church life which no one has as yet told us how to solve. It comes from our democracy. Democracy demands that the church shall acknowledge no distinctions of class. The only answer which we make to this demand is to organize churches on social lines. Watch the changes in a great city. The moment a church loses caste it begins to be unpopular. Those of a given social standing leave the community and so the church, and those of another social standing do not seem to care to come in to take what is left. I can see no way of meeting the issue except by developing such a love and loyalty and reverence for the church as will allow us to overcome even changes of locality. It is a fact that the stronger the church feeling is, the more democratic in reality the church is. An Episcopal church will usually stay longer down town than a Congregational or Presbyterian church.

I think that we must come to a deeper love for the church, if we are to make it answer its larger and more generous purpose toward men. For this reason I value all attachments to a local church. I am not so anxious as many are to see the rolls of an old church kept clean to the exact resident membership. A man has a right in the church of his father, and of his father's father. Spiritual ancestry counts for something. The old spiritual homesteads are sacred. Let us cherish them. Let us keep the identity of the best souls with them.

Why should not the churches bear the name of the saints, — our churches bear the names of our saints? What is the church, in one of its most glorious aspects, but the succession of steadfast, loyal, believing, sacrificing, conquering souls. I put the eleventh of Hebrews beside the Nicene Creed or the Westminster Confession. I put the roll of God's elect at any time beside "the form of sound words" in which they utter their beliefs. The greater souls of all generations, — they are the living church. They maintain the succession. They ennoble and enlarge the spiritual kinship. They fix the standards of faith and life. They live on from age to age to shame the selfish, the unbelieving, the faint of heart; to show willing souls how to serve, to challenge brave men to meet the possibilities of life and death. Let their names stand, to be known and read of all men, a reminder and an example of "the faith once delivered to the saints."

There are many things which I might have said of the relation of the pulpit to the church; the field is very wide. What I have said has been with the intent of turning your thoughts towards your indebtedness. If you succeed as preachers, one large factor in your success will be the acknowledged ministry of the church. If you fail, one reason of your failure will be the neglect of its strong, kind, and patient ministry.

VIII

THE OPTIMISM OF CHRISTIANITY

I AM conscious, as I bring this course of lectures to a close, how inadequate has been my presentation of those more vital aspects of preaching, which I have been trying to set forth. That preaching is a vital process from first to last I am absolutely sure. There lies its power, and there lies its weakness. Preaching rises and falls with the preacher. It is sensitive even to his moods. It is dependent upon the steadiness of his intellectual discipline, upon the nobility of his ambitions, upon the growing susceptibility of his nature to the highest inspirations. And yet we do not make sufficient account, I think, of this vital element in preaching, nor apprise the preacher sufficiently of the immense issues which are involved in the development of his personality. The preacher does not ask enough of himself, neither does society ask enough of him. We want good preaching and like it, but we do not expect it, as we ought. As Pascal says, "We go to our library and take down a book, expecting to find an author, and lo, to our joy, we find a man." We go to church expecting to hear a sermon, and lo, to our joy, it may be, we hear a preacher. The attitude of men toward the pulpit is expressed in the hope of discovery rather than in the confidence of expectation. Public sentiment at this point needs to be changed. Not that anything has come in to take the place of preaching in the public mind. There has been during the past decade a revival of the spirit of worship in the non-liturgical churches. It was greatly needed. The result has been much experimentation, but with it a large and positive enrichment of public worship. The spiritual life of the church has been quickened. There had been an earlier revival of Biblical study. The Scriptures have been searched as at no previous time in the history of the church. The spiritual life of the church has been quickened by this also. But preaching has not been rendered less necessary because of the increase of worship or of Biblical knowledge. These new influences have properly reduced the time of the sermon, but they have greatly ministered to its power. There is no religious any more than there is any secular substitute for preaching. It is the vernacular of the gospel. The language of creed or chant can never express the glad tidings as one man can tell them to another. Preaching, we say, is the soul of Protestantism; but why the soul of Protestantism unless it is equally the soul of Christianity? Let us not draw our inspiration for preaching from anything that is intermediate or formal. I like to go back in my search for first things to the saying of an old teacher in the seminary. "I teach," he said, "that Congregationalism is a passing form of Puritanism; that Puritanism is a passing form of Protestantism; that Protestantism is a passing form of Christianity."

Back in the heart of the everlasting gospel lies the necessity and the guarantee of preaching. And particularly because Christianity can get no adequate expression except through preaching. It cannot communicate itself, its spirit, its tone, its desires, its certainties in any other way. Its incentives call for the preacher. They are made to stir him. For Christianity is the revelation of a great hope as well as of a great love. There is the secret of its power. Men are saved by hope. Love that did not issue in hope would be a futile and pathetic love.

In this last lecture I want to try to make clear to you how much of the power of preaching lies hidden in the optimism of Christianity.

Whatever incentives may come to the preacher from any of the causes to which I have referred from time to time, nothing comes to him so fresh and quick from the heart of Christianity as this incentive of the great and sure hope. And Christianity is, I believe, returning to its early optimism. There have been times in the history of Christianity of sad depression, times when Christianity was not itself. There have been times when Christianity lived upon borrowed strength quite as much as upon its own. Its doctrines were not distinctive. Its language was not that of the New Testament. Its tone was not true to the life of Jesus. And there have been times when Christianity has been overshadowed by some prevailing doubt, passing under the eclipse of faith. Christianity has at such times remained true to itself, but it has not been able to communicate its spirit to the heart of the world. Men have not wanted to disbelieve, they have simply not been able to believe.

I think that no poet has caught so truly this spirit of unwilling doubt as Matthew Arnold. Listen to his lament: —

> "Oh, had I lived in that great day
> How had its glory new
> Filled earth and heaven, and caught away
> My ravished spirit too.
>
> "No thoughts that to the world belong
> Had stood against the wave
> Of love, which set so fresh and strong
> From Christ's then open grave.
>
> "While we believed, on earth he went,
> And open stood his grave:
> Men called from chamber, church, and tent,
> And Christ was by to save.
>
> "Now he is dead! Far hence he lies
> In the lone Syrian town,

> And on his grave, with shining eyes,
> The Syrian stars look down."

The religious life of the past generation has found a true, because contradictory, expression in Tennyson and Matthew Arnold. Tennyson has given expression to the strong and irresistible, but undefined hope which has held its place in our hearts; Matthew Arnold has given equal expression to the widespread, unwilling, pathetic doubt which has found its way at times within. We have been strangely confused in feeling by these alternating moods and experiences. Now it has seemed as if Tennyson's hope was the incoming tide of faith; and now it has seemed as if Matthew Arnold's doubt was the undertow which was sweeping us out again to sea. There are signs, I believe, that the confusion is passing away. We are beginning to come out into the calm assurances of Christianity. The hope which greets us is not the outcome of sentiment. It is not a reaction from past uncertainty and doubt. It has its own reasons, some of which I will bring before you, as I view the present religious experience and faith.

The tone of Christianity is determined primarily by the thought of God. Whatever the prevailing thought of God is, that, more than all things else, makes Christianity what it is in sentiment and expression. No one can fail to see that the theological discussions of the past years, except those on purely critical questions, have had to do with the nature and disposition of God, and with the methods of his working. As the result of these discussions some things are beginning to be clear.

It is beginning to be clear, as it seems to me, that we did not say the final word when we declared the change in theology from the conception of sovereignty to the conception of fatherhood. I do not know that we could have secured certain necessary results in any other way, but the result we did secure was not altogether complete and satisfying. The fatherhood of God was a satisfying conception of the personal relation of the human soul to God, especially as interpreted through the sonship of Jesus. I recall the assurance which came to my own thought when I read the confession of faith of Richard Hutton, of the London

"Spectator," as he passed over from Unitarianism into the Church of England, given in his treatise on "The Incarnation and Principles of Evidence."

God, he said in substance, is our Father because he is eternally the Father. That is guaranteed by the sonship of Christ. No new relation is created to meet the need of men. It is the same principle at work toward men in turn which had always been in the heart of God, which had its satisfaction in the eternal love of the Father and of the Son. Nothing could be more satisfying than that statement. Within the limits of its application the thought was complete.

But I really think that none of us have been satisfied altogether with the popular presentation of the thought of the fatherhood of God, as it has been applied to all the relations of God to men and to the universe. Whatever we might put into it, and say belonged there by right, others would ignore, and thus leave the conception incomplete and insufficient for the satisfaction of truth. I think that we have felt the need of a larger sense of power and determination in the attitude of God to men, greater even than could be expressed in the thought of sacrifice. And so I welcome, not the return of thought from fatherhood to sovereignty, but the advance of sovereignty into fatherhood, the incorporation, the absorption, if you will, of fatherhood into sovereignty, to give it character, and disposition, and direction. What we want to know in order to satisfy the optimism of Christianity is, not simply that God loves us, but that God is for us. We want sovereignty relieved of all doubt about its disposition and action. The idea of the fatherhood of God gave us that relief. It set sovereignty free from all limitations, free from an arbitrary election, and limited atonement, and a restricted providence. It left it "the power of God unto salvation unto every one that believeth." Now we can read the eighth of Romans, and rejoice in it. We can read it aloud, everywhere, to all men. We can read it beside the parable of the prodigal son.

And with the advance in the conception of God, the conception of his love reinforced by power, we have a corresponding advance in the conception of the work of Christ. Here again, I think, we have felt that there has been an insufficient use made of the power of Christ. His humanity has been brought to the front in every form of promise and incentive. It has been an infinite relief to turn from disputations about his work, about his atonement even, to the real Jesus as he lived, and taught, and worked, and suffered, and died. But in all our uses of the humanity of Jesus, we have not been able to fathom the meaning of his sacrifice or of the law of sacrifice which he laid down. Aid has come to us from an unexpected source. The incoming of the theory of evolution has done more, I believe, than all else to develop and solemnize the thinking of our times. For it has been a revelation or exposure of the suffering, the unconscious sacrifice, going on in all the orders and ranks of life leading up to man. And surely, though almost imperceptibly, it has been at work to change our conception of human life. It has overthrown our easy settlements of questions of human rights and human obligations. Take its influence upon the thought of man in his political relations. I quote from Professor Royce:

"The dignity of human nature under the old science lay in its permanence. Because of such permanence one could prove all men to be naturally equal, and our own Declaration of Independence is thus founded upon speculative principles, that, as they were then stated, have been rendered meaningless by the modern doctrine of evolution. Valuable indeed," he goes on to say, "was all this unhistorical analysis of the world and of man, valuable as a preparation for the coming insight; but how unvital, how unspiritual, how crude seems now all that eighteenth century conception of the mathematically permanent, the essentially unprogressive and stagnant human nature in the empty dignity of its inborn rights, when compared with our modern conception of the growing, struggling, historically continuous humanity, whose rights are nothing until it wins them in the tragic process of civilization."

We are at last beginning to have a view of the place which sacrifice holds in the development of nature, in the order of society, and therefore in the saving of man. We see in a new light the meaning of the great iterations of Jesus about the necessity of sacrifice, — words which he applied sometimes to himself, sometimes to all men. Above all, we see the necessity which lay upon him from the beginning to the end, from his temptation to his cross, to ratify this law. We see how the hope of the race was bound up in his unswerving loyalty to the principle, in that unfaltering courage which led him up to Jerusalem, in full view of the end. As the method of Jesus comes out more clearly before the eyes of this generation, we are enabled to mark its place in the law of the universe, and also to see how weak and inconsistent any other method would have been, and therefore to realize how great and sure is our hope of its success in the spiritual salvation of the world.

And in like manner there has come to us a clearer understanding of the power of the spirit of God in the world, as manifest in the continuity of God's working. We have been led, perhaps I may say forced, to recognize the universality of the work of the spirit of God, its work in all times and all places. We have been reading history not only with a larger intelligence, but with a broader faith and a wider spiritual vision. Great spaces in history, whole ages, that were blanks have been filled in with God's plans and with his presence. And although we have not been able to apportion all things aright, we have been able to see, if not compelled to believe in, the continuity of God's working. Doubtless we have not yet gained the full perspective. The mystery of the world is not solved. What we call providence does not always take the course to be expected, or even, as we thought, to be desired. The Christian believer may still cry out with Lessing, " Go Thine inscrutable way, Eternal Providence. Only let me not despair of Thee because of Thine inscrutableness. Let me not despair in Thee even if Thy steps appear to me to be going back. Thou hast on Thine Eternal way so much to carry on together! so much to do! so many side steps to take!"

And yet some things are plain and sure.

The great plan itself is growing plain and sure, and more glorious to the Christian intelligence and faith. It is becoming more evident that there is a divine order in the world. And the tone of Christianity is changing with the larger and clearer apprehension of the fact. This is the first reason which justifies the present optimism of Christianity. It has its rational support and incentive in the conception of sovereignty as directed and applied by the hand of love, of sacrifice as the law of the universe, of the divine order, as seen in the continuity of God's working.

But Christianity takes its tone also at a given time from the particular truth or doctrine upon which stress at the time is laid. The incoming truth of to-day brings in with it, perhaps above all other distinctive Christian doctrines with the exception of the doctrine of immortality, the element of hopefulness. It is the truth of the kingdom of God, the kingdom of God on earth. I refer now to the doctrine, not to the fact. The incentive to hope always lies in the truth, more than by any possibility it can ever lie in the fact. It is the ideal which stirs us to faith. We keep our eye on the goal, even though it be, as has been said, a flying goal.

The truth of the kingdom of God has always existed. It has been an inseparable part of Christianity. Jesus preached it. He made it central in his preaching. But it has never had the separateness and distinctness of a doctrine. It has never found its way into our articles of faith in any specific form. We have not tried to formulate it, as we have formulated the doctrine of the person of Christ, or of human nature, or of the church, or even of the last things. And I do not know that we are trying to formulate it now. But somehow the truth is here. It is in men's thoughts, it is on their lips, it is stirring at their hearts.

You may see the negative effects of its power in our present conceptions of the church. How small and petty our separations and divisions are beginning to seem, our denominations and sects, in the light of that broader and more comprehensive idea which has taken possession of our minds. One must either secularize the church as the Romanist usually does, or reduce it to technicalities as the ritualist does, to get any satisfaction out of mere churchisms. We are all trying to get together on the spiritual, the ethical, and the intellectual side. We work together in surprising ways, and we think together, or at least we think above the separating lines. We do not reason any longer by denominations. We reason as scholars, or as workers, or as preachers. Church unity is not a fact; perhaps it never will be. But Christian unity is a great deal more of a fact than it was twenty years ago, ten years ago, one year ago. It now begins to have dimensions. You can point to it. Anybody can see it.

But the special fact to which I wish to call your attention is the courage which is taking possession of the church at large under the incoming of this truth. The courage to which I refer is seen in the new objects which Christianity is seeking to gain. Christianity began with the conversion of individuals. It has always been and always will be the divine work of Christianity to save the individual soul. Protestantism gave a mighty impulse to that work, but it inheres in Christianity. This is not so much a matter of courage as of patient and sacrificing love. The courage of Christianity came out more clearly in the conception of the modern missionary. It was still the thought of individual salvation. Souls in heathen lands were the objects of search and rescue. But gradually the idea grew and enlarged itself into that of the saving of the lands themselves. It finally comprehended tribes and peoples and races.

The present advance is more courageous still. Christianity is now aiming at the forces which make up civilization, to purify, control, and direct them. If there has been any loss of interest in missions it is due, I think, very largely to this transfer of interest to the various forces of society and state which need to be more thoroughly christianized. Christianity is becoming mightily concerned about Christendom. We are beginning to understand, we have been suddenly awakened to, the sense of what I call the inevitableness of Christianity as a power in the world. The Christian nations are moving under an irresistible momentum. Nothing can be so impressive as to stand in the presence of a great moral law when it is operating on a grand scale. Such a law is now in operation all over the world. It is the law which Christ enunciated: "To every one that hath shall be given, and he shall have abundantly, and from him that hath not shall be taken away even that which he hath." Under the working of this law the transfer is now being made from lower civilizations to higher, as before it had been made from pagan to Christian. It is in some ways a sad spectacle which we are now witnessing, — old nations breaking up, old races losing place, and new nations and races advancing and coming upon them, often in the spirit of greed and competition, to gather the spoils. While the process was going on in Africa we gave little heed to it. Now that it is at work in Asia, on a larger scale and before venerable races and civilizations, it is startling and appalling. But it is inevitable. The law will work, but it may be made to work in Christian as well as in unchristian ways.

And now it has come to us. The great national and international question which has been so suddenly thrust upon us, and which has so sobered the nation, is this same question of the inevitable transfer of power from the lower civilization to the higher, from the less Christian to the more Christian. We cannot escape the law. We cannot delay it beyond its time. But the responsibility of seeing that it works in a Christian way is our responsibility, like that of England or of any other Christian nation in the East. It is this responsibility which is now giving us pause. It is this which sobers us. We are not acting in the haste or indifference which comes of the spirit of greed. We feel something of the solemnity which comes to one who is a part of an inevitable situation. We begin to understand that it may be as solemn a thing to gain as to lose, to be the one to whom it shall be given as to be the one "from whom it shall be taken, even that which he hath."

And yet all these changes and transfers are a part of the problem which Christianity has created. It has made a new world.

It has changed in every way the balance of power. When Mommsen dates modern history from the transfer of power from the Mediterranean to the Atlantic, he gives also the ground of the change which was to mark the moral advance of the world. Christianity is in the blood of the races which are in power. And the courage of the church lies in the fact that Christianity is now beginning to deal with its own creations, with its own institutions and laws and industries, in the endeavor to set them right. It is a greater work than that of evangelizing the world, though no more sacred. It is a part of the threefold problem, which Dr. Hitchcock used to say was always present to Christianity, — to keep, to gain, to recover. Christianity has dropped a nation or a race here and there on its westward march. These must be recovered, like the peoples won from its grasp by Mohammedanism. It is at the same time seeking the remoter peoples of India, Japan, China. It must still keep those in hand, the peoples of Europe and America.

It is at this last point that the problem is

evidently the closest. Christianity is mightily congested at the modern centres, London, Paris, Berlin, New York, and the forces with which it has to deal are more difficult to control than those which confronted the old civilizations. Modern civilization introduces its own forces, having their seat in the market, which are quite as strong as those which raged on the field of war. Turn which way we will, the emphasis falls on some situation in the kingdom of God. Every form of spiritual activity, every method of material advancement, every new movement of a people or a race, brings the idea to the front. We cannot escape it. We are not trying to escape it. It is the inspiring truth which is now gathering in the consciousness of the church, and is being distributed through the consciousness of the individual preacher to react upon his personality.

I can call your attention to but one other reason for the present optimism of Christianity.

The tone of Christianity at a given time depends altogether upon those who are most responsive to its claims. Where is

Christianity making its strongest appeal today? Upon whom in our generation does the appeal fall with the greatest recognition? Where is the spirit of consecration the readiest, and the most urgent? I should say that in a peculiar degree, and within a wide range, Christianity had laid hold upon the younger life of our time.

It is a very important question with any organization, Does it have its available force within call? The most available force of the church lies in the generation which has time before it sufficient for a given plan. Movements which affect the future of the church and society usually originate with young men, not because they are more inventive or necessarily more earnest, but because they have time to carry them out. There is a manifest awakening to-day in that generation of the church which has time for carrying out its plans. It may be too much to say that plans have been formed. It is not too much to say that desires and ambitions have been quickened. I put in evidence the various groups which largely gather up the incoming life of the church in its various parts, — the Society of Christian Endeavor, the Brotherhood of St. Andrew, the Students' Volunteer Movement, and the movement toward College Settlements in the great cities, which though not in all cases distinctly of the church is dominated by the religious spirit — these, and their equivalents in the different communions, Protestant and Catholic. I might add to this evidence the testimony, in some cases the unexpected testimony, of those who have to do with our educational and religious institutions as to the seriousness and earnestness of the incoming generation. I have no hesitancy in affirming, within the limits of my observation, the promise of greater moral power in the generation preparing for action than is to be found in that now in action.

This movement all along the line starts from the common principle of consecration, and converges, or can be made to converge, toward some end for the betterment of humanity. Something of this result is doubtless due to the change of emphasis on the part of the church from experience to consecration, a change which some may deprecate. It is but fair to state that the teachings of the church were formerly repressive rather than directive, tending to introspection rather than to action; but that does not materially lessen the value of the fact with which we are concerned. That fact is, let me repeat it in another form, the heroic is not far off. There is, on the part of the better life in training, a growing sensitiveness to human conditions. There is a growing responsiveness to ideals of duty. Perhaps it may have no sufficient outcome, but if such be the result, it will be the first disappointment of the kind in Christian history.

The tone of Christianity is that of perpetual youth. It is unnatural when Christianity cannot incorporate the optimism of youth into its own optimism. Not every age has succeeded in making this incorporation. Our age has succeeded in a marvelous degree. Its success constitutes in a great part its religious enthusiasm. It gives an inspiring spectacle. Just as it is pathetic to see a generation passing away, lamenting its unfinished work, losing heart because it has failed in its plans, so it is inspiring to see a generation come in with undaunted hope, and with eager hands, to take up its own tasks and carry them on to a hoped-for completion. The new generation may make no greater relative advance than the old, but like each which went before it has the joy of its service and of its hope.

I am grateful in your behalf that as you enter upon this vital process which determines the making or the unmaking of the preacher, your age is on the whole with you and not against you. You must find your encouragement as you look about you, perhaps as much outside the ministry as within. I should not say that this was peculiarly the age of the preacher; but it does belong by its greater incentives, its inspirations, its discoveries, its responsibilities, by all things which go to make up its sober optimism, to the preacher as much as to anybody. More to him than to anybody if he has the insight and courage of a noble faith.

I have been speaking to you to-day about the atmosphere of Christianity in which you begin your work. I believe that it is charged with hope. I have given you my reasons for my faith. The generation, as you are better able to feel it than any one else, is alive. You are not taking up the unfinished task of old men, written over with failure. You belong to a generation which is taking the initiative, proposing to itself new methods and new ends. You have the rare advantage of watching a new truth as it begins to take shape in the thought of the church, no less a truth than that of the kingdom of God, a kingdom of righteous forces, as well as of righteous men and nations. And you have above all the readjusted thought of God set with new power to the needs of men; the sovereignty of God, transformed and transfigured by his fatherhood; the cross of Christ acknowledged as the supreme example of the sacrificial law of the universe; and the assurance of the divine order, the continuity of the divine working, made manifest by the recognized presence of the spirit of God as a universal presence.

This is the present phase of the optimism of Christianity, some part of which we must feel to be the preacher's. I do not know that Christianity ever came to an age with a larger hope or a better faith. It may be many and many an age before He shall come to whom the kingdoms of the earth belong, and whose right it is to rule, but surely we may take up in confident faith and urge on its way the great prayer of the Puritan statesman and poet who caught the hope and expectation of modern Christianity, the Christianity not only of men, but of nations.

"Come forth out of thy royal chamber, O Prince of all the kings of the earth; put on the visible robes of thy imperial majesty; take up that unlimited sceptre which thine Almighty Father hath bequeathed to thee: for now the voice of thy bride calls thee, and all creatures sigh to be renewed."

www.ingramcontent.com/pod-product-compliance
Lightning Source LLC
Chambersburg PA
CBHW021826230426
43669CB00008B/878